LOST GARDENS OF
GERTRUDE JEKYLL

LOST GARDENS OF GERTRUDE JEKYLL

Fenja Gunn
With Illustrations by the Author

Macmillan Publishing Company
New York

Maxwell Macmillan International
New York Oxford Singapore Sydney

Macmillan Publishing Company
866 Third Avenue
New York, NY 10022

Macmillan Publishing Company is part of the Maxwell Communication
Group of Companies.

Library of Congress Cataloging-in-Publication Data

Gunn, Fenja.
  Lost gardens of Gertrude Jekyll / Fenja Gunn.
    p.   cm.
  Includes index.
  ISBN 0 – 02 – 546516 – 3
    1. Landscape gardening. 2. Flower gardening. 3. Landscape
gardening — England. 4. Flower gardening — England. 5. Jekyll,
Gertrude, 1843 – 1932. I. Title.
SB473.G86 1991   91 = 11003
712' .6—dc20   CIP

Macmillan books are available at special discounts for bulk
purchases for sales promotions, premiums, fund-raising, or
educational use. For details, contact:

Special Sales Director
Macmillan Publishing Company
866 Third Avenue
New York, NY 10022

10   9   8   7   6   5   4   3   2   1

Printed in Hong Kong

FRONTISPIECE: Marksdanes Spring Borders

Contents

For my Parents

Introduction

'WHEN THE EYE is trained to perceive pictorial effect, it is frequently struck by something – some combination of grouping, light and colour – that is seen to have that complete aspect of unity and beauty that to the artist's eye forms a picture. Such are the impressions that the artist-gardener endeavours to produce in every portion of the garden.' Thus Gertrude Jekyll introduced her chapter on 'Some Garden Pictures' in *Colour in the Flower Garden*, one of her most influential gardening books.

The analogy between painting and gardening is one which Jekyll made frequently in her writing. During the course of researching this book, I have been constantly aware of her extraordinary ability to form 'garden pictures' in her mind, translating these into planting plans which would later become 'a series of enjoyable pictures painted with living flowers'. Not the least astonishing aspect of this aptitude was the prolific nature of her genius. By the time Jekyll died, she had been involved in the design of about 350 gardens over a period of forty years.

A visitor to one of these gardens, who had studied its plans, would in all probability be confronted by a scene which would be greatly different from his expectations. The Jekyll garden would have disappeared, replaced by its successor. Our informed visitor might imagine the garden as Jekyll wished it to be planted: a mass of lavender here, flanking steps that led upwards, perhaps tree heaths at a higher level and then woodland with shrubberies of rhododendrons. But this could only exist in the imagination of the onlooker, for in most of Jekyll's gardens today little of her original planting remains. The truth is that the great majority of her gardens are simply lost gardens. And it was from these lost gardens that the idea came for this book. Although the gardens no longer existed, the 'garden pictures' of Jekyll's imagination might be brought to life in paintings.

My aim has therefore been to try to recreate a small but representative selection of Jekyll's garden plans by watercolour paintings that show her gardens as they were intended to be planted. I have chosen plans that cover every facet of her work, including her grand planting schemes and individual specialised features. I have also shown interesting details of design, planting and colour for individual borders and Jekyll's favourite plant and colour combinations. The paintings seek to illustrate Jekyll's imagination, not only as a remarkable garden designer and plantswoman but also as an artist who, through a poignant accident of fate, was forced to choose the ephemeral medium of plants for her pictures rather than a conventional palette of paints.

I have also sought to give this book a practical dimension. Jekyll's colour schemes, specialised features and grouping of plants still have a relevance for any gardener, even if one does not have a Jekyll garden to restore. Although I would not advocate recreating a Jekyll garden where one was never intended, individual details and features, particularly her colour combinations of plants, can still have a place in today's gardens. Accordingly, each watercolour painting is accompanied by a detailed planting plan which gives contemporary and, if these have changed, present plant names. Since many of Jekyll's plants are no longer available, even from specialist nurseries, I have suggested, under the guidance of horticultural experts, alternative plants or varieties as close to the original as possible, with the emphasis on similarity of colour. This substitution can only be approximate because some plants, for example many iris hybrids, have now been bred with a different genetic composition from those which Jekyll used.

So much can still be learned from one of our finest garden designers and related to our own gardens. Many of her exceptional effects, created with a bold, simple use of plants, are not so hard to reproduce and Jekyll, never a plant snob, devised even her most elaborate schemes with a mixture of plants which included many familiar cottage garden favourites.

My interest in Gertrude Jekyll began when I read her books and collections of articles on plants and gardening. She appeared to be that rarity, a knowledgeable plantswoman and practical gardener with the talent to communicate in writing a passion for plants and deep love of gardens. I was intrigued to discover more about her background. Two biographies, by Betty Massingham and by Jekyll's nephew, Francis Jekyll, told the story of this remarkable woman. Coming from a comfortably off middle-class family, as a young woman she had taken the daring step of enrolling herself at the Kensington School of Art. Even with an artistic mother, who may have been sympathetic with her daughter's ambition to become a painter, this was an unusual break with tradition for a respectable girl in Victorian England.

But her talent was not reserved for painting alone. Witty and intelligent, she soon began to move in artistic circles and could number among her friends many well known painters and such influential artists and thinkers as William Morris and John Ruskin. Her travels with cultured friends in the near East and in Europe stimulated her mind and artistic senses. She developed an interest in a variety of crafts as diverse as wood-carving and silverwork, furnishings and embroidery, and at all these she exhibited skill and talent.

A move from Berkshire back to her childhood county of Surrey coincided with an increasing involvement in plants and gardens. She met and became friendly with William Robinson and contributed to his journal, *The Garden*. The influence of his gardening philosophy was to determine the course of her own developing ideas about planting and design. At this time Jekyll may have thought that gardening was to be yet another acquired skill with painting remaining her prevailing interest. But the close work involved in painting and in her crafts put a constant strain on her weak eyesight. She frequently suffered from severe headaches through eye strain and was eventually forced, in her late forties, to consult a famous eye specialist. His gloomy prognosis dashed her hopes of continuing her work as a painter and her favourite craft of embroidery was also discouraged.

Any artist can imagine what Jekyll suffered, suddenly deprived of her lifelong interest and ambition. But she was not to be daunted. Fortified by a deep Christian faith and her own strength of character, she transferred her developed skills as a painter and embroiderer – her ability to compose a picture, her sensitivity to colour and appreciation of different textures – and applied these to the art of gardening. It is no accident that the metaphors she uses throughout her horticultural writing are those of painting and drawing: she constantly refers to creating 'garden pictures' and the work of the 'artist-gardener' or 'garden artist' and her eye for colour when grouping plants together was the result of an art education and familiarity with a palette of paints. Jekyll continued to design gardens until the year of her death. When she died aged 89, she had been involved in the design of about 350 gardens from around 1890 to 1932. Sadly, only 220 plans, often incomplete, of these gardens survive, rescued from possible oblivion by the American landscape designer, Beatrix Farrand, who bought them at a sale and eventually, after her death, bequeathed them to the University of California.

I became curious to discover what had happened to Jekyll's gardens, particularly those less well known and created outside her celebrated partnership with the architect, Edwin Lutyens. Fortunately, her plans are now kept at the College of Environmental Design, University of California and are also on record at the Royal Commission for Historical Monuments in London. Having studied the many rolls of film which cover the only remaining evidence of her work, I decided to do some historical detective work to try to find out the state of at least a few of these gardens today. I soon realised how little remains of Jekyll's planting and that many of the garden sites have been divided up or built over. Few Jekyll gardens in Britain have been accurately restored and only one garden in America is at present undergoing a programme of planting to accord with its original design. I came to the conclusion that the only way in which these lost gardens could be brought back to life was by recreating them in paintings. It also seemed to me that this would not be inappropriate since Jekyll, according to her own planting philosophy, would have visualized her plans as 'garden pictures'. Creating a picture of a garden in her imagination would also have been necessary because, after 1900, she was not willing to travel further than a few miles from her home at Munstead Wood, Godalming, in Surrey, to visit her clients' gardens. Her poor eyesight and love of her home surroundings made her reject all attempts, even by the most distinguished clients, to persuade her to design gardens on site. She relied on her developed senses as an artist, combined with a wide knowledge of plants, to compensate for the fact that she did not actually see most of the gardens that she planned. This makes her achievement as a designer all the more remarkable.

I decided to select twenty gardens and to research in detail each site of my choice. My object was to try to illustrate these in paintings which, I hoped, would capture something of the character and intention of Jekyll's designs. I attempted to visualize each garden as Jekyll might have imagined it when it was fully planted and matured.

Visiting the gardens of my choice, I felt, would provide me with a framework and setting for my paintings. I set myself the task of discovering the background and history of each garden to establish its identity within the context of Jekyll's work. This would also enable me to explore the working relationships between Jekyll and her clients.

I based my selection of gardens initially on the amount of information available in the

II. A formal garden layout for shrub borders, Chart Cottage (see Chapter Four)

plans. It was essential to decipher Jekyll's planting plans as fully as possible before I could attempt a painting of any garden, for I would have to convert a flat plan marked out with planting areas into a painting of the garden shown in relief, with each group of plants in its proper place. Jekyll's writing was frequently illegible and, in addition, the identification of her choice of plants was often difficult because she used her own abbreviated descriptions of them. Plant names too have changed over the years: to identify two familiar examples, 'megasea' on Jekyll's plans is now bergenia and 'laurustinus' has become *Viburnum tinus*.

I wanted my choice to cover a wide range of Jekyll's designs and to include both grand and modest gardens so that the breadth of Jekyll's work could be appreciated. I subsequently discovered that often the smaller, apparently less challenging commissions revealed as much of Jekyll's skill as her larger and more obviously inspiring schemes. Having made my selection of gardens, I wrote off to 'the Owner' in the hope of getting a response. To my delight, I began to receive replies from most of the present owners of the gardens.

The next stage of my background research involved seeking material from every available source. Although Jekyll relied principally on plans, relief drawings and measurements provided for her by architects and surveyors who were planning a site, she also conducted detailed correspondence with her clients. The information that many clients produced gave a clear picture of the sites, and written details were often supplemented by photographs and little sketches. For most of the gardens I have chosen there are letters which relate to their design, and I have included extracts in my text. In a few cases, the correspondence is missing, or else letters proved unnecessary because

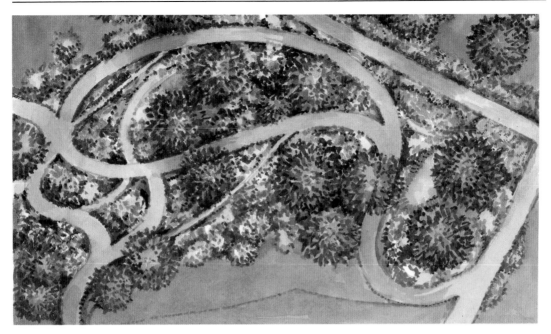

III. An informal layout of paths in woodland, Walsham House (see Chapter Twelve)

the garden's proximity to Jekyll's own home enabled her to visit the site. Some clients were invited by Jekyll to come and discuss their plans at Munstead Wood and this had the advantage of allowing them to see what she had achieved in her own garden.

The relationship between designer and client has always depended on the personalities involved. Some of Jekyll's clients approached her with undemanding enthusiasm; others were more business-like. These clients were frequently in a hurry to have an instant garden and Jekyll, in common with many garden designers today, had to satisfy this demand for a quick effect by producing schemes which were often over-planted. It may also explain why she sometimes proposed a temporary scheme using annual plants before she drew up the final plan for permanent planting.

Visiting the gardens which I have chosen for this book has been one of my greatest pleasures in putting the work together. Apart from the kindness and hospitality I was shown by the present owners of the gardens, I have constantly felt privileged to visit sites which, in many cases, Jekyll never saw herself. The condition of these gardens varies but, in all cases, most of the original planting has disappeared with the passage of time. I was able to identify trees, some old shrubs and fine examples of hedging, but Jekyll's herbaceous planting has been lost. This is hardly surprising since only one of the gardens which I have included in the book has remained under the care of one family. Most have had several changes of owner, often with long periods of neglect in between when the property remained unoccupied. Plants have a limited life and elaborate planting schemes need to be maintained by a large team of gardeners: such a skilled and adequate labour force is rarely available today.

My choice of title for the book describes the present state of Jekyll's planting schemes in all but one or two of her gardens. As the gardens in this book are a representative cross-section of Jekyll's commissions, they reflect the prevailing loss of her planting schemes. However, this does not prevent the gardens from remaining interesting examples of Jekyll's work and, in many cases, their present owners have sensitively maintained their character. One of the delights of my visits has been to discover some fine original feature or hard landscaping in a garden layout that was recognisable from Jekyll's plans. It is good to report that, at the time of writing, three of the gardens in this book are being restored to their original design, including Jekyll's planting.

My decision to choose a particular Jekyll plan for one of my paintings was ultimately determined by the qualities of the garden design itself; but, as an additional bonus, my research unearthed many intriguing facts about the gardens of my choice and these made each garden come alive and assume its own distinctive identity. The gardens have been chosen from all over Britain, from Somerset in the South to an island off the mainland of Scotland in the North. I have also attempted to recreate two of Jekyll's three American gardens, a cottage garden in Connecticut, at present being restored, and a site in Ohio with an ambitious design which was never implemented. In many cases I found myself telling owners for the first time that theirs was a Jekyll garden. I even had to convince one owner over the telephone by giving an exact description from Jekyll's plan of the garden: scepticism was finally dispelled when I described the precise design of a flight of steps leading down from a terrace.

During my research it became evident that many of Jekyll's plans for her clients were never realised on the ground. Some of these planting schemes are included in my selection of gardens: they are still relevant as examples of Jekyll's work and are 'lost gardens' in the most exact sense. It is understandable, for a variety of logical reasons, that some of Jekyll's plans were not carried out. My own belief is that many were not implemented because Jekyll felt unable to visit the sites herself. The plans she produced were often elaborate and presented the kind of problems that could have been more easily resolved on site. The relationship between designer and client is an extremely sensitive one and the kind of specialised gardening knowledge which Jekyll possessed could not have been readily imparted to her client by the architect or surveyor involved on the site. The fact that Jekyll was not able, in person, to convince anxious clients that a planting scheme would work as well on the ground as it did on paper, or to brief their head gardeners, meant that many of her ideas were probably abandoned.

So Jekyll started with a severe disadvantage before she even began to design a garden. She had to rely on information which was gathered for her by others and was often confronted by the problems of working on plans for a garden which she had not seen. In common with most garden designers, Jekyll repeated her favourite plants, colour schemes and features. It was particularly necessary, in her case, to discover successful formulae for her garden designs to compensate for the fact that she might not visit each site and was therefore unable to identify its individual problems. It must be acknowledged that in these cases she would not have been readily able to absorb and appreciate the garden's own special sense of place. No amount of factual information from the most co-operative client could have easily replaced this last intangible but important missing ingredient in her design work.

The style of design which she developed was based on many of the ideas tried and tested in her own garden at Munstead Wood. There she had the leisure to observe, plan and plant over the seasons. This invaluable trial ground and her own extraordinary ability to visualize a planting scheme in her imagination allowed her to overcome problems which a lesser designer and artist would have found insurmountable.

My visits to the gardens illustrated in this book and my study of the plans produced for them established for me that Jekyll's formulae for design and planting substantially overcame the handicaps I have mentioned and worked with exceptional success for a variety of sites. Most of her gardens were based on a formal plan, with terracing, pools and the shaping of lawns and borders contributing to the formality of the layout. Within this disciplined structure, Jekyll's bold drifts of planting and ingenious use of colour would have appeared all the more rich and exuberant. Although apparently complex on paper, the actual effect that was achieved was never fussy. By planting in generous swathes and with a carefully controlled blend of colours, Jekyll harmonised the plants with their setting.

Formal layout provided Jekyll with a strong framework for her planting: planning informal gardens without seeing the site was more difficult. Jekyll's rock gardens, which often incorporated natural pools or streams, or her woodland walks, which required subtle landscaping, would have been harder for her to visualize. They required 'the artist's eye for balance and proportion' and might be thought impossible to realise on paper alone. But Jekyll, once again, used an often-repeated and successful formula. She devised layouts which had no straight lines, in contrast to her formal gardens, but were based on a curved network of paths weaving their way round islands of planting. The shapes were drawn with confident draughtsmanship establishing a disciplined framework for her planting.

Each of my paintings is based on the research I have described. I have taken great care to reproduce the garden settings for my paintings as authentically as possible. I have also made every effort to reproduce the colours of plants accurately. In some cases I have had to rely on a verbal description only, as the plants in question are no longer grown and I have not been able to trace any visual reference. Where this has occurred, I have sought to blend the colour of the plant into the harmony of the garden's complete colour scheme. The planting in the borders and gardens has not been painted with the precision of botanical illustrations: my aim has been to produce paintings which make the gardens come to life and, therefore, it has been essential for me to visualize the garden as a whole and not as a series of individually drawn plants.

I have done my best to transmute the 'garden pictures' Jekyll might have imagined into watercolours of her gardens. My overriding aim has been to evoke the spirit of every garden I have painted and to recapture something of its former glory. Even if the full splendour of her planting belongs to a past age, Gertrude Jekyll's work can still be a source of inspiration.

Chapter One

Full Colour Borders

J EKYLL'S IMAGINATIVE SCHEMES for herbaceous borders were among her most daring
contributions to garden design. Not only do these borders demonstrate her
comprehensive knowledge of a wide range of plants; they are also an example of her
ability as a 'garden artist' to paint with plants. The schemes were meticulously planned
and Jekyll implemented a sequence of colours based on carefully conceived principles.
The final effect was to create a garden picture on a grand scale. Perhaps the exercise of
planning it relieved Jekyll of her frustration as a painter who could no longer work with
a conventional palette of paints.

These colour sequences were inspired both by an emotional response to colour and
by a desire to implement an intellectually conceived theory well known to artists of the
day. As a craftswoman and painter, Jekyll would have been familiar with M. E.
Chevreul's definitive scientific work on colour harmonies and on the relative effect of
adjacent colours. Chevreul, a talented chemist, became Director of Dyes for the
Gobelin Tapestry Works and it was his detailed research into colour dyes which led to
the development of his theories. Jekyll directly refers to one of Chevreul's experiments
when she describes the effect of complementary colours applied to the planting in a
border: 'The brilliant African Marigold has leaves of a rather dull green colour. But
look steadily at the flowers for thirty seconds in sunshine and then look at the leaves.
The leaves appear to be bright blue'. Her use of white flowers to unify a colour scheme
may also have been inspired by Chevreul's directive that 'all primary colours gain by
their juxtaposition with white'.

Chevreul related his theories to both painting and tapestry and his ideas were familiar
to the Impressionists who experimented with blends of colour in spots and swirls of
paint. The Neo-Impressionists who used *pointillist* techniques, building up a picture in
tiny dots of paint, were influenced by Chevreul's experiments with adjacent colours of
tapestry threads, so that their finished paintings were almost a weave of colours. Jekyll,
in turn, was influenced and inspired by these painters just as she had been receptive, as
a young painter, to Turner's innovative use of colour and his approach to colour
harmony.

Thus Jekyll drew on these influences when she set out to design herbaceous borders
and, with the ground as her canvas, she used her wide knowledge of plants, their
variety of textures and colours, their cultural requirements and flowering seasons, to
create a rich and beautiful but intellectually conceived picture in plants. Her description
of her own hardy flower border at Munstead Wood was a perfect example:

The planting of the border is designed to show a distinct scheme of colour arrangement. At

IV. Watlington Park Double Herbaceous Borders

Watlington Park Herbaceous Borders (page 15)

1. Gypsophila = *Gypsophila paniculata*.
2. Galega = *Galega officinalis*.
3. *Polemonium alba (P. caeruleum album)*.
4. Liatris = *Liatris callilepsis* or *L. spicata*.
5. *Aster* 'E. Goodman' [variety untraced].
6. White hollyhocks.
7. Fan-trained peaches.
8. Stachys = *Stachys olympica* (syn. *S. byzantina*).
9. *Campanula carpatica*.
10. Yellow snapdragons.
11. Tradescantia = *Tradescantia* × *andersoniana*.
12. Primrose African marigolds.
13. *Buphthalmum salicifolia*.
14. *Rudbeckia newmanii (R. fulgida speciosa)*.
15. Hollyhock 'Pink Beauty', in left border. Unspecified pink hollyhocks in right border.

16. *Helenium pumilum*.
17. *Heuchera micrantha*.
18. Gaillardia.
19. Tall dark snapdragons = dark red.
20. *Artemisia lactiflora*.
21. White dahlia.
22. Red hollyhocks.
23. Cleome = *Cleome spinosa*.
24. Snapdragon 'Orange King'.
25. Orange African marigolds.
26. *Polygonum bunonsis (P. affine)*.
27. *Geum* 'Mrs. Bradshaw' *(G. quellyon* 'Mrs. Bradshaw').
28. *Helenium autumnale*.
29. *Rudbeckia* 'Golden Glow' *(R. laciniata* 'Golden Glow').
30. Tritoma (Kniphofia)
31. Megasea (Bergenia = *B. cordifolia*).
32. Red dahlias.
33. Continuation of left-hand border plants already listed and drifts of: Calendula sown in border, monarda, *Lychnis chalcedonica*, *Pyrethrum uliginosum (Leucanthemella serotina)*, erigeron, *Phlox* 'Elizabeth Campbell', pink, centred flower [* *P. paniculata* 'Sandringham': ◊ 'Eva Cullum'], *Anemone japonica*, statice = *Statice latifolia (Limonium latifolia)*, delphiniums, sidalcea, dicentra.
34. Continuation of right-hand border with plants already listed and drifts of: Calendula sown in border, *Heuchera richardsonii* [* *H. americana*], *Coreopsis lanceolata*, *Helenium striatum*, gold and crimson, [* *H. hoopesii* 'Red and Gold': ◊ *H. autumnale* 'Riverton Beauty' or *H. a.* 'Gartensonne' which grows up to 6ft/1.8m], *Phlox* 'Mrs. Oliver', salmon pink, dark centre [* *P. paniculata* 'Bright Eyes', 'Bill Green': ◊ 'B. Symons-Jeune'], *P.* 'General Van Hentz', orange-scarlet [* *P. paniculata* 'Brigadier': ◊ 'Orange Perfection'], *P.* 'Avalanche', white [* *P. paniculata* 'White Admiral', 'Rembrandt': ◊ 'Mt. Fuji'].
35. *Clematis flammula*.

the two ends there is a groundwork of grey and glaucous foliage... With this, at the near or western end, there are flowers of pure blue, grey-blue, white, palest yellow and palest pink; each colour partly in distinct masses and partly inter-grouped. The colouring then passes through stronger yellows to orange and red. By the time the middle space of the border is reached the colour is strong and gorgeous... Then the colour-strength recedes in an inverse sequence through orange and deep yellow to pale yellow, white and palest pink; with the blue-grey foliage. But at this eastern end, instead of the pure blues we have purples and lilacs... Looked at from a little way forward, ... the whole border can be seen as one picture, the cool colouring at the ends enhancing the brilliant warmth of the middle (*Colour in the Flower Garden*).

Jekyll was annoyed when a visitor, passing along her flower border with its ingeniously arranged colour scheme, remarked in criticism of his own gardener's current efforts at herbaceous planting: 'I told my fellow last autumn to get anything he liked, and yet it is perfectly wretched. It is not as if I wanted anything out of the way; I only want a lot of common things like that' (*Wood and Garden*). But perhaps this should have been taken as an unintended compliment to Jekyll's planting because its effect was so harmonious and apparently so simply achieved that, like many fine works of art, it appeared artless.

My first example of Jekyll's designs for herbaceous borders has been chosen from the gardens of Watlington Park in Oxfordshire. Set high up in the Chilterns with spectacular views over the flat Oxfordshire plain, Watlington Park is a handsome, classical Georgian house in mellow brick with pediment and detailing in stone. The building is set among five acres of gardens, surrounded by natural woodland, facing a swathe of open parkland with fine mature trees. The formal gardens extend all round the house and these, although Edwardian in character, are perfectly in harmony with the house.

I visited the gardens on a bright, early autumn morning. The clarity and sharpness of the light showed off the gardens and their layout to advantage. The spacious lawns planted with trees and shrubs lead away from the house towards an orchard and wild

An explanation of the plant lists

Plant names are listed in the keys to the garden paintings as they appear on Jekyll's plans. Current plant names are enclosed in brackets. A brief colour description is given of plant varieties that are no longer available. * indicates currently available alternatives to older contemporary plants specified on Jekyll's plans: ◊ indicates currently available American alternatives to those same plants. For annual plants and for dahlias, consult current nursery and seed catalogues for a colour match.

Jekyll did not always specify the variety of a plant she intended to be planted. In some cases, where the choice of alternatives is limited, I have offered my own suggestions for a variety of plant, e.g. Gypsophila = *Gypsophila paniculata*. The quantity of plants Jekyll included for each drift of planting was always extremely generous. Where space on a site was limited, she would have used a few different plant varieties but each drift would have included a number of individual plants.

V. Hursley Park Herbaceous Border

A long herbaceous border which was planned to run the length of a kitchen garden wall at Hursley Park in Hampshire. The planting was designed in a carefully planned colour sequence, beginning with cool colours represented by lavender, grey-leaved stachys, white and pink

phlox and snapdragons, and then building up to a climax of yellow, orange and red in the centre of the border. Here Jekyll used kniphofia, scarlet monarda, dark red snapdragons, African marigolds and nasturtiums. The painting shows that, as the planting recedes from view, the colours of the plants return to the cool pastels which began the sequence. A variety of blue and purple flowers ends the border.

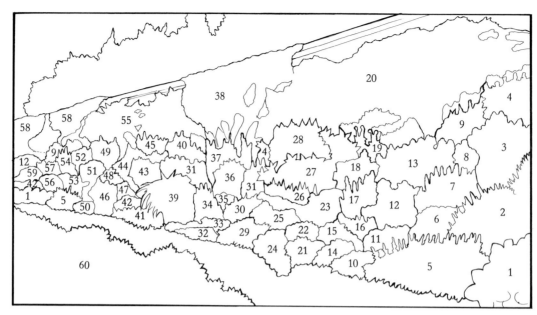

Hursley Park Herbaceous Border (pages 18–19)

1. Megasea (Bergenia = *B. cordifolia*).
2. Lavender = *Lavandula angustifolia*.
3. *Phlox* 'Avalanche', white [* *P. paniculata* 'White Admiral', 'Rembrandt': ◊ 'Mt. Fuji'].
4. White dahlia.
5. Stachys = *Stachys olympica* (syn. *S. byzantina*).
6. Pink scabious = variety of *Scabiosa atropurpurea*.
7. Tall pink snapdragons.
8. *Lavatera trimestris* sown in border.
9. *Pyrethrum uliginosum (Leucanthemella serotina)*.
10. Pink *Phlox drummondii*.
11. *Dicentra eximia*
12. *Chrysanthemum maximum*.
13. *Phlox* 'Elizabeth Campbell', pink, centred flower [* *P. paniculata* 'Sandringham': ◊ 'Eva Cullum'].
14. Scarlet *Dianthus heddewigii*.
15. Double rose godetia sown in border.
16. Pink stock = *Matthiola incana*.
17. Dark snapdragons = dark red.
18. Scarlet monarda = *Monarda didyma* 'Cambridge Scarlet'.
19. *Dahlia* 'Oldfield Bedder' [untraceable].
20. Peach.
21. Dwarf French marigolds.
22. *Linum grandiflorum*.
23. Orange African marigolds.
24. Yellow tropaeolum = *Tropaeolum majus*.
25. *Helenium pumilum*.
26. Dwarf tritoma (kniphofia).
27. *Ricinus* 'Gibsonii' (*R. communis* 'Gibsonii').
28. Japanese striped maize = Variegated *Zea mays*.
29. White gazania.
30. *Catanache caerulea*.
31. Tall pale yellow snapdragons.
32. Variegated mint.
33. *Phacelia campanularia*.
34. White snapdragons.
35. Primrose African marigolds.
36. *Lilium candidum*.
37. *Delphinium belladonna* = belladonna variety.
38. *Clematis flammula*.
39. *Glyceria aquatica (G. maxima* 'Variegata').
40. *Anchusa* 'Opal' (*A. azurea* 'Opal').
41. *Polygonum bunonsis (P. affine)*.
42. *Collinsia bicolor*.
43. Giant white gladiolus.
44. *Eryngium* × *oliverianum*.
45. *Artemisia lactiflora*.
46. Snapdragon 'Mauve Queen.
47. White stock.
48. *Iris sibirica*.
49. Echinops = *Echinops ritro*.
50. Dwarf ageratum = *Ageratum houstonianum*.
51. *Eryngium giganteum*.
52. *Campanula persicifolia*.
53. Deepest purple China aster.
54. *Delphinium consolida* – larkspur, sown in border.
55. Nectarine.
56. *Scabiosa* 'Azure Fairy' (*S. atropurpurea* 'Azure Fairy').
57. *Salvia virgata (S. virgata nemorosa* [syn. *S.* × *superba*].
58. *Clematis jackmanii*.
59. *Scabiosa caucasica*.
60. Rose beds [roses unspecified].

garden which provide a link between the cultivated grounds and woodland. A generous sized kitchen garden enclosed by high brick walls occupies an area on one side of the formal gardens, and between this and the house is a large circular tank surrounded by opulent, well-kept yew hedging. Philip Tilden, the architect probably responsible for the overall layout of the gardens, also produced the designs for the charming garden house sited close by. A raised tennis lawn on the other side of the house enhances the Edwardian flavour of the gardens. The grounds have benefited from having remained under the care of one family, but nothing much of Jekyll's planting remains as the gardens have been simplified for ease of maintenance. The yew hedging, however, and some of the mature trees and shrubs are original and the gardens still retain the layout that appears on Jekyll's plans.

Watlington Park is the home of the Esher family and in 1922, Viscount Esher and his wife commissioned Jekyll to produce a scheme for the gardens. Twelve plans are still in existence and there are also photographs of the original garden. These were sent to Jekyll to provide her with a setting for her planting designs.

Antoinette Brett, Viscount Esher's wife, wrote detailed letters to Jekyll describing the features of the gardens that she felt needed changing. She wrote critically about the current design of her gardens: 'The garden as it is at present lacks flavour, character, a little I think'. The herbaceous borders were of particular concern: 'You will see [referring to a plan of the garden she has sent to Jekyll] that there are two long borders in the kitchen garden, and two more down below running parallel... the other two double borders are too much alike – yet I quell at the thought of pulling out all these plants. You see I really have a great deal of stuff, much of it bought last year, and I cannot very well cast it aside. What do you advise?' She mentions a list of the plants that she is sending to Jekyll in the hope that Jekyll will incorporate these plants into her new plan for the borders.

I have chosen to paint the borders designed to be planted outside the kitchen garden with the high brick wall on one side and the orchard and wild garden beyond. Nothing remains of the original herbaceous planting today and the gravelled path which once ran in between the borders is now grassed over. But this continues to provide an attractive walk between the mellow brick outside wall of the kitchen garden, still peppered with pegs once used to secure peach trees to the brickwork, and the strip of orchard which appears to have many old varieties of apple.

The herbaceous borders were about 140 ft (43 m) long and were divided in the middle by a pathway which led into the kitchen garden through a gate. Jekyll adopted her favourite colour formula for the planting of these borders, with cool blues at either end and a crescendo of brilliant colour in the centre. I have shown the borders at the height of summer in August when the effect of the planting would have been at its most dramatic. The borders are painted receding from sight with the flowering plants in the distance seen as a mass of dots of colour like a *pointillist* painting. The gateway which frames the borders still exists today and, from the viewpoint of this picture, the wall on either side of it masks the foreground end of the borders. The planting here begins with a predominance of blue plants, the start of a sequence of cool colours. *Aconitum napellus*, echinops, nepeta and scabious are Jekyll's choice for this position with a generous drift of *Stachys olympica* to edge the pathway on either side. White hollyhocks, dahlias, polemonium and gypsophila, with its clouds of tiny white blooms, are mixed in with the blue flowers to produce an even cooler effect.

As the sequence moves into warmer colours, tall hollyhocks in pink and red stand at the back of the borders with dahlias in between. Splashes of gold and yellow are provided by rudbeckia, helenium, buphthalum, calendula, French and African marigolds and snapdragons. White flowers punctuate the border throughout, enhancing the rich colours of the other blooms. The dividing pathway cutting centrally through the borders is flanked by generous clumps of kniphofia which add their bright torches and architectural form among the less disciplined plants. Beyond this the borders recede in a mass of flower colour.

My second example of a herbaceous border was produced by Jekyll for Hursley Park in Hampshire. Hursley Park is a substantial eighteenth century house which once belonged to the Heathcote family. In 1902 the estate was bought by Mr. G. A. Cooper, a solicitor from Elgin, Morayshire, and his wife, a wealthy American. The Coopers already had an estate in Scotland and a large London house and had the funds to donate a valuable park and house to Cooper's home town of Elgin. They proceeded to implement extensive alterations to their newly acquired house. At one stage, four hundred workmen were at work on the site, many of these being skilled craftsmen whose work was recorded in photographs for an article in *Country Life*, in 1909.

During the First World War, the grounds of Hursley Park were used as the Divisional Headquarters of the 8th Division and the second floor of the house was used as a hospital. Between the wars the house and its occupants returned to a normal life and in 1925 Jekyll was commissioned to produce her designs for the gardens; twelve of these plans still remain. With the death of Sir George Cooper in 1940 and the outbreak of the Second World War, Hursley Park was requisitioned by Lord Beaverbrook for Vickers Aviation Ltd. whose premises in Southampton had been bombed. It was at Hursley Park that Vickers developed one of their most famous aircraft – the Spitfire. In 1958 the house and grounds were acquired by IBM for their development laboratories.

The gardens were in a derelict state when IBM took over but they restored the sunken garden with its Italianate pool and handsome pergola and, although no Jekyll plans exist for it, this part of the gardens is typical of many which appear in her plans. Where there are no buildings, the grounds have been landscaped or replanted and the many fine mature trees already well established in the gardens are now monitored by computer to make sure they remain in good condition and free from disease. I could discover nothing remaining of the kitchen garden which Jekyll was to redesign for the Coopers and I belive that its site is now built over with offices and other functional buildings. This was where the magnificent herbaceous border shown in Jekyll's plans was to have been, but now only these plans and, fortunately, correspondence remain as evidence of its existence.

Lady Cooper wrote to Jekyll: 'I am venturing to write and ask if you ever visit gardens to give advice in regard to them as if so it would give me great pleasure to see you here and I shall be so very grateful for advice in regard to my herbaceous borders which I cannot get successfully planned'. Clearly, Jekyll observed her usual rule and did

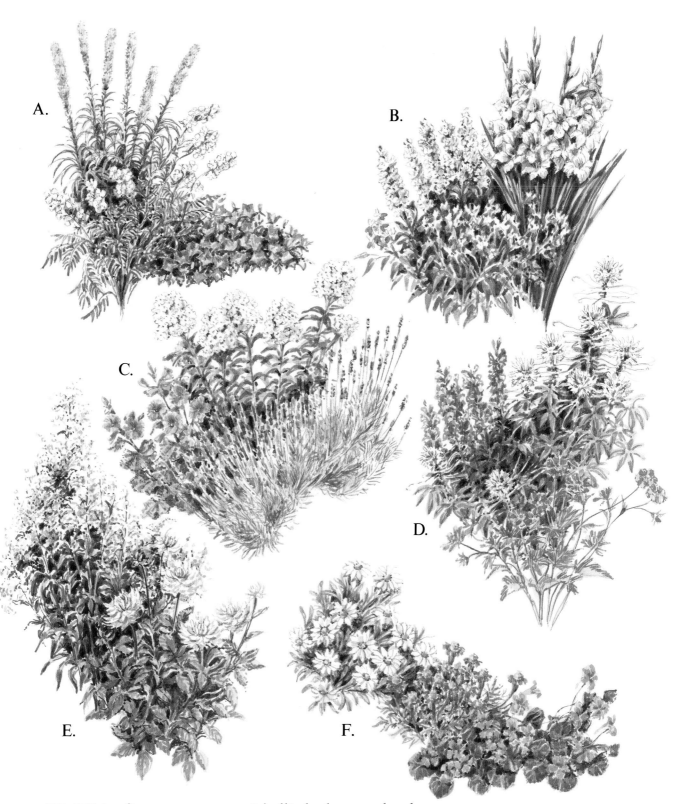

VI. White flowers punctuate Jekyll's herbaceous borders.

A. *Polemonium caeruleum album, Liatris callilepsis, Campanula carpatica.*   **B**. White gladiolus and stocks, *Collinsia bicolor.*   **C**. White phlox, lavenders, *Lavatera trimestris.*   **D**. *Cleome spinosa, Geum quellyon* 'Mrs. Bradshaw', dark red snapdragons.   **E**. White dahlias, *Artemisia lactiflora.*   **F**. White gazania, dwarf French marigolds, nasturtiums.

not visit the Coopers, otherwise it would not have been necessary to obtain so much detail of the gardens through correspondence. Jekyll corresponded with Lady Cooper (she spelt her name 'Cowper') and her husband, although he evidently left details of planting to his wife who made it clear in one of her letters to Jekyll that 'I am very fond of the rather old-fashioned flowers, and of sweet smelling things; and I am extremely anxious to get really good colour effects... Also perhaps you could give me a hint or two about the herbaceous border – I should be most grateful for it as I do want to get something as lovely as possible'. Apart from the design for this border, Jekyll also produced a series of beds with limited colour schemes including a blue and mauve border, a yellow and bronze border and one exclusively planted with blue plants.

The long herbaceous border which ran below a high brick wall in the enclosed kitchen garden at Hursley Park is a good example of one of Jekyll's grand herbaceous borders. Jekyll questioned Lady Cooper in detail about the soil conditions of the proposed border and it was agreed between them that the soil was 'stiffish'. I was puzzled when I first looked at Jekyll's plan because the wall appeared to be left bare except for two groups of clematis; but the correspondence reveals that the wall was planted with peaches and nectarines. Jekyll asked her client: 'As you are away in August and September do you wish the best plants for these months to be omitted? This would be Dahlias, Hollyhocks, Tritomas, Helianthemum and the larger half-hardy annuals such as the showy French and African marigolds'. Lady Cooper was obviously anxious not to limit the scope of Jekyll's plan because she asked to have these plants considered for the final design and, in the result, there are a large number of annuals and half-hardy annuals in this border.

Jekyll has used a wide variety of plants to achieve her colour effect. The two ends of this long border, in the front row of plants, are marked by generous plantings of *Bergenia cordifolia, Stachys olympica* and lavender. In between these two groups are a fine array of dwarf plants – campanulas, phlox, dianthus – and a mass of low growing cottage garden annuals such as ageratum, nasturiums and marigolds. Behind these plants were stocks, snapdragons in pinks, yellows and white, taller varieties of French and African marigolds, pink godetia and scabious, pink *Linum grandiflorum*, bright daisy-like helenium, and a large clump of white *Chrysanthemum maximum* beyond which were massed two groups of *Phlox paniculata* – the pink 'Elizabeth Campbell' and a white variety named 'Avalanche'. Tall blue delphiniums stand at the back of the border in the centre next to *Anchusa azurea* 'Opal'. Planted on either side there are white delphiniums, dahlias and *Chrysanthemum uliginosum* (syn. *Leucanthemella serotina*).

Jekyll also included plants which introduced a sculptural effect and added foliage interest to this fine display of summer flowers. The spiky foliage of iris and gladioli, also in bloom at this time, the torches of dwarf kniphofias and a group of tall architectural white lilies, probably *Lilium candidum*, stand out among the more exuberant plants. To these are added coppery *Ricinus communis* 'Gibsonii', striped Japanese maize, a typical Jekyll choice, and a generous clump of *Glyceria aquatica* which proves that the soil must have been heavy and certainly moisture-retentive. A spread of variegated mint all adds to an effect that was varied and colourful. Jekyll also mentions a 'French' amaranthus which was to be sown, I imagine as a form of underplanting, round the stems of some of the tall plants at the back of the border. I have discovered that this was a dwarf annual variety *Amaranthus sanguineus* 'Nanus', not apparently available today, supplied to Jekyll from Paris.

The final garden in this chapter provides another example of double herbaceous borders like those planned for Watlington Park. But the length and scale of these borders are reduced to fit a modest sized garden. Hill Top is an attractive Edwardian family house in Guildford with a garden arranged on different levels overlooking the Surrey landscape. The views are spectacular, particularly as, even today, there are few buildings to be seen. The better known Jekyll garden, Highmount, which features in *Gardens for Small Country Houses*, by Jekyll and Lawrence Weaver, is sited nearby. Jekyll designed her plans for her client, Mrs. Walter Neall, in 1921 and eight plans remain of the scheme for Hill Top. The garden is only an acre in size but is cleverly designed to make the most of its site. It still retains the layout designed for it by Jekyll but, although the garden is richly and variously planted so that it remains full of charm and interest, the original planting has mostly disappeared. Nevertheless, as I went round the garden with the owner, we spotted clumps of *Acanthus spinosus* in exactly the position planned for it by Jekyll.

The present owner was only made aware that she owned a Jekyll garden in 1985. Before she bought the house the property had remained unoccupied for a long time. During this period the garden had been neglected and, although the owner believes that the garden had once contained a wide variety of plants, many of these had obviously disappeared with the passage of time. The elaborate terracotta vase which features in a drawing by Jekyll is also missing, although its stone plinth still remains. The date which was on the vase, 1638, makes me think that Jekyll had either sketched an antique piece which had been acquired for the garden or had drawn the original vase so that a copy of it could be made.

The borders which I have painted are no longer planted out as Jekyll planned, nor are they edged with the little box hedges which I have shown. However, these are still present elsewhere in the garden as edging to shrub borders. A planting of box midway down the herbaceous borders could well be an original planting as it occupies the precise position allocated for it on Jekyll's plans.

I have shown the borders in August, viewing them from a high level so that most of the plants can be seen. The parallel borders were designed to be viewed from the house and were placed so that they appeared framed in the middle of a window. They ran across the garden between two levels making the most of a long clear stretch. Jekyll repeated this layout in many of her smaller gardens, thereby creating an illusion of spacious elegance in a restricted area. On the left-hand side of the borders behind the beech hedge, the garden drops and then levels out providing an area for borders. This drops again to another level which is screened from the road by a yew hedge. The magnificent views of Surrey lie beyond.

On the right-hand side of the picture there is a planting of shrubs which separates the herbaceous borders from the highest level of the garden, laid out as a tennis lawn. The borders run between a beech hedge on one side, which is still in existence, and shrub planting on the other side. A gravel path in the centre divides the borders. Halfway down the path there is a break in the borders, allowing space for a seat on one side of

VII. Hill Top Herbaceous Borders and Octagonal Garden

Jekyll planned these double herbaceous borders in 1921 for a garden in Guildford. They were designed to be seen from the house framed in a window. The planting is shown as it would have appeared in August, an exuberant display of summer colour, enclosed by a hedge on one

side and shrubs on the other. The borders break in the middle to allow space for a seat on the right facing a terracotta vase mounted on a stone plinth which is shown on the left of the painting. Low box hedges edge the borders, and the gravel path which divides the planting leads to a small grassed octagonal garden enclosed by hedging.

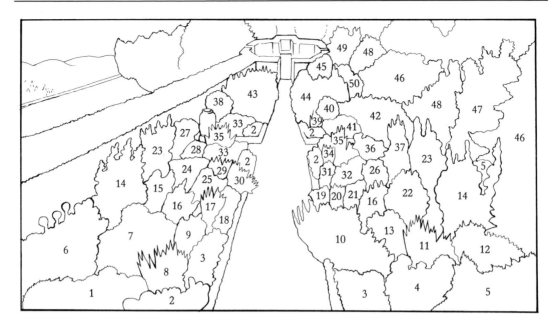

Hill Top Herbaceous Borders and Octagonal Garden (pages 26–7)

1. Santolina = *Santolina chamaecyparissus*.
2. Megasea (Bergenia = *B. cordifolia*).
3. Stachys = *Stachys olympica* (syn. *S. byzantina*).
4. *Scabiosa caucasica*.
5. Savin (*Juniperus sabina*).
6. Echinops = *Echinops ritro*.
7. *Artemisia ludoviciana*.
8. Iris [unspecified] in two purples.
9. Polemonium = *Polemonium caeruleum*.
10. Nepeta = *Nepeta* × *faassenii*.
11. Iris = tall bearded iris – 'Kharput'.
12. Aster [illegible].
13. Erigeron.
14. White hollyhocks.
15. *Phlox* 'Avalanche', white [* *P. paniculata* 'White Admiral, 'Rembrandt': ◊ 'Mt. Fuji'].
16. Pink snapdragons.
17. Iris = tall bearded iris – 'Queen of May', pink/red self [* 'Rosy wings', 'Susan Bliss': ◊ 'Playgirl', 'Priceless Pearl', 'Adventuress', 'Pearly Shells', 'Lace Jabot', all soft lilac-pink].
18. *Campanula carpatica*.
19. Dicentra = *Dicentra eximia*.
20. Iris = tall bearded iris – 'Mrs. H. Darwin' or 'Darius'. Darius, a blue/yellow bicolour [* 'Golden Alps':◊ 'Lullaby of Spring', 'Bold Accent', 'Tequila Sunrise', 'Sostenique']. 'Mrs. H. Darwin', white with inconspicuous violet veins [* use 'Bridesmaid', white: ◊ 'Lacy Snowflake', 'Laced Cotton', 'Pontiff', 'Leda's Lover', 'Skiers Delight', all white]
21. Gaillardia.
22. *Pyrethrum uliginosum* (*Leucanthemella serotina*).
23. Pink hollyhocks.
24. *Isatis glauca* [* *I. tinctoria*].
25. Buphthalmum = *Buphthalmum salicifolia*.
26. Dark snapdragons = dark red.
27. *Anemone japonica*.
28. *Campanula macrantha* (*C. latifolia*).
29. Iris = tall bearded iris – 'Multicolor', yellow bicolour [* 'High Command', 'Staten Island', 'Rajah': ◊ 'Rising Moon', 'Aztec Treasure', 'Love the Sun', 'City of David'].
30. Polygonum = *Polygonum bunonsis* (*P. affine*).
31. Snapdragon 'Orange King'.
32. Montbretia (Crocosmia).
33. Monarda = *Monarda didyma*.
34. *Iris flavescens* – bearded yellow flag iris.
35. Tritoma (Kniphofia).
36. Centranthus = *Centranthus ruber*.
37. Red hollyhocks.
38. Helenium = *Helenium autumnale*.
39. Iris = tall beared iris – 'Sans Souci', red bicolour [* 'Grace Sturtevant', 'Queechee', 'Solid Mahogany': ◊ 'Chocolate Shake', 'Cayenne Pepper', 'Hell's Fire', 'Play with Fire'].
40. *Lychnis chalcedonica*.
41. Centaurea = *Centaurea montana* or *C. cyanus* – cornflower.
42. Fuchsia = *Fuchsia magellanica* 'Gracilis'.
43. Continuation of left-hand border with drifts of: *Lychnis chalcedonica*, African marigolds, *Helenium pumilum*, *Glyceria aquatica* (*G. maxima* 'Variegata'), *Campanula persicifolia*, Spiraea

(continued opposite)

the pathway with a plinth opposite on which stood the terracotta vase. I cannot be absolutely certain about this siting of the vase but a square plinth base is clearly marked in this position on Jekyll's plans with a circle on top of it representing the base of a vase or urn. I also feel that the choice of plant colours in the borders on either side of the vase would have complemented perfectly the warm tones of terracotta. The path continues beyond this point and leads the eye on to a most distinctive and unusual feature. This is an octagonal garden, laid out to grass and enclosed by hedging. There is an alcove for a seat from which, in this cool and quiet green setting, one could sit and enjoy the exuberance of the herbaceous borders at the height of summer.

Jekyll indicates a low hedge edging these herbaceous borders and, since box forms part of the shrub planting, I have assumed this to be box hedging. The planting begins at the near end of the borders as they appear in my picture with soft silver-grey and grey-blue foliage plants – santolina and *Artemisia ludoviciana*. These cool tones are picked up by the flower colours of nepeta, echinops, *Scabiosa caucasica*, *Campanula carpatica* and erigeron. At the back of the borders stand tall hollyhocks in pink, white and red, and at the far end of the right-hand border *Clematis flammula* has been trained to climb over delphiniums which have finished flowering. The cream of the clematis blooms is seen again in the perennial meadowsweet, *Filipendula ulmaria*. White flowers punctuate the borders: *Chrysanthemum maximum*, *Anemone japonica*, phlox, pinks, hollyhocks and snapdragons. The centre of the borders is marked by a blaze of colour: the flaming-torches of kniphofia, orange red montbretia, scarlet *Monarda didyma*, and *Lychnis chalcedonica*, golden helenium and calendula and a mass of French and African marigolds and orange snapdragons. These surround, in a generous swathe on either side, the plinth with the terracotta vase. The seat facing the vase is flanked by fuchsias and, as Jekyll has not specified these, I have chosen one of her favourite hardy fuchsias, *Fuchsia magellanica* 'Gracilis'. The pink of the fuchsia flowers is part of a pink theme running through the borders with polygonum, valerian (*Centranthus ruber*), tall pink snapdragons and hollyhocks.

The whole colour scheme is typical of Jekyll and is enhanced by the green surroundings of the hedge on one side and the shrubs on the other: a mixture of box, ribes, forsythia and *Chaenomeles speciosa* with *Viburnum tinus* (her favourite 'laurustinus') and laurel at the far end of the borders. Finally, there is the cool green octagonal garden to which the herbaceous borders lead the eye.

venusta (Filipendula rubra), tall bearded irises 'Bronze Beauty' [* 'East Indies', 'Lord Warden', 'Louvois': ◊ 'Bronze Fawn', 'Copper Classic', 'Trails West', 'Cable Car'], 'Vincent', blue bicolour blend [* 'Amigo', Wabash', 'Braithwaite': ◊ 'Proud Tradition', 'Best Bet', 'Glistening Icicle', 'Nordic Seas', 'River Hawk'; or 'Persian Gown', purple bicolour], hollyhocks, delphiniums, snapdragons, calendula and variegated mint.
44. Continuation of right-hand border with drifts of: montbretia (crocosmia). *Iris* 'Florentina', tall bearded-iris 'Celeste', blue self [* Jane Philips,

Harbor Blue, Patterdale: ◊ 'Sapphire Hills', 'Tide's In', 'Song of Norway', 'Lake Placid', 'Carved Crystal', 'Olympiad', 'Victoria Falls'], *Chrysanthemum maximum, Spiraea ulmaria (Filipendula ulmaria)*, pink and white pinks, anchusa, delphiniums, snapdragons and hollyhocks.
45. *Clematis flammula.*
46. Box = buxus.
47. Ribes.
48. *Pyrus japonica (Chaenomeles speciosa).*
49. Forsythia.
50. *Berberis aquifolium (Mahonia aquifolium).*

Chapter Two

Colour Combinations

THE PLANTS which Jekyll chose for her colour schemes were for her the equivalent of an artist's palette of paints. But although the individual colours might be beautiful or striking in their own right, their true value lay in their relationship to each other on the canvas. In her introduction to *Colour in the Flower Garden* Jekyll wrote: 'Having got the plants, the great thing is to use them with careful selection and definite intention. Merely having them, or having them planted unassorted in garden spaces, is only like having a box of paints set out upon a palette. This does not constitute a picture'.

Jekyll used a comprehensive spectrum of plant colours to create her garden pictures. She planned blends and harmonies within each colour range. Silver and grey merged into grey-blue, violet-blue and purple to produce a continuous colour sequence, and the introduction of palest yellow or white flowers among the blues served to emphasize their cool mysterious quality. Pale cool pink, lilac, violet-pink and deep pink gradually changed into yellow, orange, red and claret thus building up into a blaze of hot colours at the centre of a border.

The paintings in this chapter show groups of plants taken from herbaceous borders described in this book. I have tried to show a typical sequence of colours and tones starting with the silver and grey foliage of *Stachys olympica*, *Artemisia ludoviciana* and *Santolina chamaecyparissus*. The soft grey of the stachys provides a subtle foil for the lavender-blue flowers of *Nepeta* x *faassenii* and *Scabiosa caucasica*. Silver artemisia and santolina complement the steely blue globular flower-heads of *Echinops ritro*. The blue sequence gives way to purple, pink and white. The velvety foliage of purple sage contrasts with the narrow silver leaves and white funnel-shaped blooms of *Convolvulus cneorum* and with a mass of pink dianthus. The two groups of plants which follow are combinations of pink flowers. Godetia and stocks (*Matthiola incana*) are planted together with *Dicentra eximia* to create a delicate blend of pinks, and tall pink hollyhocks (*Althaea rosea*) combine with valerian (*Centranthus ruber*) and *Fuchsia magellanica* 'Gracilis' to provide a harmony of deeper pink tones. White flowers are a constant element in Jekyll's planting schemes and the cool sequence ends with a mixture of white flowers: *Lilium candidum* and *Chrysanthemum maximum*, combined with pink snapdragons (antirrhinum), and white *Gypsophila paniculata* planted with pale blue *Tradescantia* x *andersoniana* and yellow snapdragons (see page 34).

The sequence of warm colours begins with a combination of tall *Verbascum olympicum* and the spreading shrub *Senecio greyi*. Both plants have yellow flowers and their combined foliage creates an appealing harmony of soft greys. A contrast in foliage shapes is the distinctive feature of the next group of plants, but it is the blend of

VIII. A cool colour sequence of plant groups

A. *Stachys olympica, Scabiosa caucasica, Nepeta* x *faassenii*   **B.** *Artemisia ludoviciana, Echinops ritro, Santolina chamaecyparissus*   **C.** *Convolvulus cneorum*, purple sage, rock pinks   **D.** Godetia, pink stocks, *Dicentra eximia*   **E.** Hollyhocks, *Centranthus ruber, Fuchsia magellanica* **F.** *Chrysanthemum maximum, Lilium candidum*, pink snapdragons

yellows, found in the lily-shaped blooms of the hemerocallis, in the bright rays of *Buphthalmum salicifolium* and in the variegated leaves of a drift of thyme, that carries the warm colour sequence through to the next group of plants. Here the yellows begin to take on a golden tone with *Rudbeckia fulgida*, *Helenium pumilum* and yellow African marigolds (*Tagetes erecta*). In the following group yellow turns to orange and orange-red with clumps of crocosmia and kniphofia, a plant so frequently used by Jekyll in her planting schemes that she simply identified it on her plans by the letter 'T' for tritoma, the contemporary name for kniphofia. Orange-red tiger lilies (*Lilium tigrinum*), scarlet *Monarda didyma* and yellow *Oenothera fruticosa* form the next group of plants followed by bright red *Lychnis chalcedonica*, yellow coreopsis and orange African marigolds. Red and bronze end the sequence with two annual plants: bronze-leaved *Ricinus communis* 'Gibsonii' and a canna which also has bronze foliage and exotic scarlet flowers.

The colour sequence shown through these paintings covers only a small but nevertheless typical variety of plants used by Jekyll to create her herbaceous planting schemes. Once she had planned a sequence, building it up to a climax of rich warm colour in the centre of a border, she had the inverse sequence to plan. Mere repetition of exactly the same groups and drifts of plants in the second half of a herbaceous border would never have satisfied such an ambitious and subtle designer. She chose either different varieties of plants to carry the inverse colour sequence through to its end or, where she repeated the same plants, placed them next to new neighbours in different quantities and positions, thus avoiding the effect of a mirror image of the first half of the border.

The greatest diversity in Jekyll's choice of flower colours lay in her selection for the plants at the cooler end of the colour spectrum. Jekyll's herbaceous borders in this book provide a good example. The variety of flowering plants in the silver to pink colour range exceeds those used to span between yellow and red. It is evident that Jekyll took a particular delight in soft colour schemes, in the 'quiet harmony of lavender and purple and tender pink, with a whole setting of grey and silvery foliage' (*A Gardener's Testament*). She also found a particular challenge in planning exclusively blue planting schemes, although she stressed that the pure blue found in certain delphiniums, and in cornflowers and anchusa, required the close proximity of white or pale yellow flowers to achieve the most striking effect.

In choosing from a variety of cool blue flowers in the lavender to purple range, Jekyll made her selection from a wide range of flower shapes: the steely blue globes of echinops and teasel-like heads of *Eryngium planum* and *Eryngium* x *oliverianum* set amongst their collars of spiny bracts, the rosettes of *Scabious caucasica*, *Catanache caerulea* and cornflowers, the bells of campanula, the delicate little saucer-shaped flowers of the perennial geraniums, *Geranium himalayense* and *Geranium ibericum*, and the hoods of *Aconitum napellus* and *Aconitum japonicum*, a tall pale-blue variety, sadly no longer available. The closest equivalent to *Aconitum japonicum* today would be *Aconitum wilsonii* with its large hoods of amethyst-blue. Another characteristic choice was the hyacinth-flowered shrubby clematis, *Clematis heracleifolia* 'Davidiana'.

Jekyll used a variety of blue annuals among the perennial plants to extend the flowering season of the border; these included familiar cottage garden plants like ageratum and blue China asters (callistephus), the pretty blue marguerite, *Felicia amelloides*, and distinctive subjects like the Californian *Collinsia bicolor* and Mexican *Commelina coelestis* with its flowers of perfect pure blue.

Many of the pink flowers featured in the herbaceous borders in this book were also annuals: *Lavatera trimestris*, pink stocks, godetia, tall pink hollyhocks and snapdragons. Tall pink and also pale yellow snapdragons were among Jekyll's favourite annuals for herbaceous borders. She grouped them on her plans in great drifts weaving in between other plants where they would provide colour all summer long.

Liatris, erigeron, dicentra, sidalcea, valerian and *Malva moschata* were among the perennial plants Jekyll used in the violet-pink to pink colour range. She also chose many pink and violet varieties of *Phlox paniculata* (then named *Phlox decussata*) from among the large number, both self-coloured and with contrasting centres, listed in contemporary nursery catalogues. Violet-blue 'Le Mahdi' is still available today, but other varieties have not survived and these include 'Elizabeth Campbell', coral pink with a deeper pink centre; 'Mrs. Oliver', salmon pink with a white centre; 'Dr. Charcot', white with a violet centre; and the tall, early flowering 'Antoine Mercier', a white variety with lilac-grey petal margins.

The warmer colour range was represented by a variety of rayed flowers: helianthus, helenium, rudbeckia, coreopsis, buphthalmum and gaillardia. These bright flowers, which seem to epitomize the optimism of hot summer days, are less fashionable today. They were an essential element in Jekyll's herbaceous borders, although some of her clients asked her not to include sunflowers (helianthus) in her planting plans because 'they are so common'. Jekyll responded with the riposte: 'Nothing is "common" in the sense of base or unworthy if it is rightly used' (*Colour in the Flower Garden*). But many of the sunflower varieties that she recommended are no longer available. These include her favourite tall helianthus, 'Miss Mellish', with its large golden-yellow flowers. Among the other rayed flowers which she recommended, *Helenium autumnale striatum*, a handsome giant with gold and crimson flowers and the shorter variety, *Helenium autumnale cupreum*, which Jekyll described as 'wall flower coloured', are both no longer grown but *Helenium pumilum* and *Coreopsis lanceolata* are still available.

The colour combination of yellow, orange and red, which included such a diversity of flowering plants – kniphofia, monarda, crocosmia, penstemon, lychnis, dahlias and cottage garden plants like nasturtiums and French and African marigolds – and formed the warm heart of Jekyll's herbaceous borders, was a difficult mixture of plants and colours to handle successfully. The margin between a splendid show of vibrant colour and vulgar garishness was a narrow one. For a less skilful designer than Jekyll it was easy to over-step and this may have been why the distinguished plantsman, Edward Bowles, recommended caution when using Jekyll's *Colour in the Flower Garden* as a reliable guide to planting: 'This book has been responsible for many an overcrowded, gaudy jumble of flowers believed to be a colour scheme, and sometimes called a Jekyll Border' (*Journal of the Royal Horticultural Society, 1937*).

One of the difficulties of planning such a colour scheme may have been the inaccuracy of contemporary seedsmen's colour descriptions, a problem identified by Jekyll herself when choosing China asters for her own garden. But for those who were prepared to implement Jekyll's plans as she had directed, or to adapt this blend of colours and plants with sensitivity and discretion, the reward could be a richly beautiful display of colour.

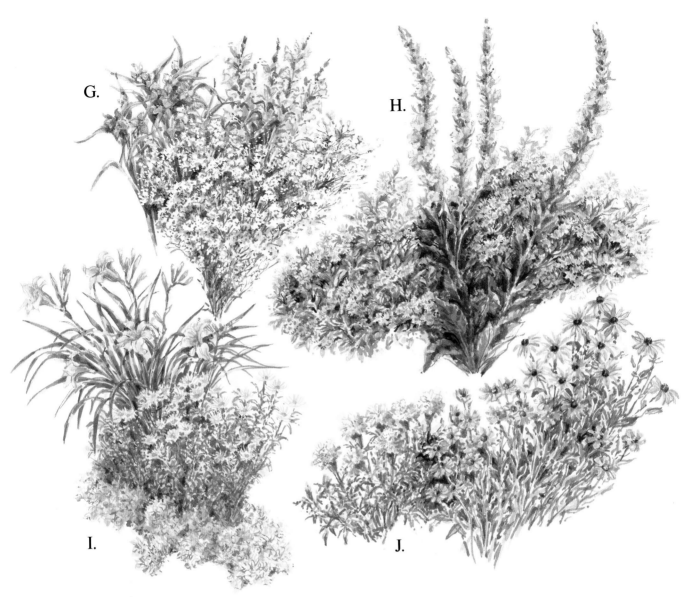

IX and X. A warm colour sequence of plant groups

G. *Tradescantia × andersoniana, Gypsophila paniculata,* yellow snapdragons.   **H.** *Verbascum olympicum, Senecio greyi.*   **I.** Yellow hemerocallis, *Buphthalmum salicifolium,* golden thyme. **J.** *Rudbeckia fulgida speciosa, Helenium autumnale* 'Pumilum Magnificum', yellow African marigolds.

Jekyll relied on white or cream flowers, and pastel colours, to separate groups of plants that would otherwise have produced a clash of colours. Her use of elegant white *Lilium candidum* to punctuate a border was a typical feature of her design. White *Campanula persicifolia,* the shasta daisy *Chrysanthemum maximum,* and clouds of white gypsophila were used for the same purpose. She chose from a wide variety of white flowers so that their different shapes and forms – the large clover-like flowers of *Cleome spinosa,* the clustered flower-heads of *Achillea ptarmica* and the abundant rosettes of white pinks – stood out with luminous clarity among the other flowers.

Plants which produced a foam of cream blooms, the perennial meadowsweet *Filipendula ulmaria, Aruncus dioicus* and *Artemisia lactiflora,* seemed to have had a particular appeal for Jekyll, perhaps because they had the effect of softening and

K. Crocosmia, kniphofia.   **L.** Tiger lilies, monarda, *Oenothera fruticosa.*   **M.** *Lychnis chalcedonica,* yellow coreopsis, orange African marigolds.   **N.** Red canna, *Ricinus communis* 'Gibsonii'.

diffusing the colours of adjacent flowers, thus ensuring a harmonious effect.

It must be taken into account that, in some cases, the colours of certain plants have changed since Jekyll's day. This is particularly true of the tall bearded irises which she used throughout her planting schemes: today's varieties have been bred with brighter colours, and their standards and falls are often more ostentatious.

Jekyll's imperfect sight may have had one compensating effect when she planned colour schemes for her own garden. Her limited area of vision, one supposes, allowed her to see colour at any distance in general shapes and areas, abstracted from the detail of its garden context. Perhaps this enabled her, when she came to design on paper, to visualize large areas of flower colour as if they were generous brush strokes of paint combining on a canvas to create a picture.

Chapter Three

Limited Colour Borders

'IT IS EXTREMELY INTERESTING to work out gardens in which some special colouring predominates, and to those who, by natural endowment or careful eye-cultivation, possess or have acquired what artists understand by an eye for colour, it opens out a whole new range of garden delights' (*Colour in the Flower Garden*). Jekyll enjoyed the challenge of creating an artistic and refined effect by limiting her use of colours.

The first garden in this chapter, the blue and mauve borders at Hursley Park, can claim to be what Jekyll referred to as a 'garden of special colouring'. The second garden at Rignall Wood is also at the cool end of the colour spectrum but a wider range of colours – blue, mauve, pink, creamy white and grey – are involved in its design. By contrast, Little Cumbrae is an example of Jekyll's use of strong, rich colours at the hot end of the spectrum: this is a red and gold garden. The final painting in this chapter returns to soft colours – rose pinks, blues and white – which were Jekyll's choice for a child's garden at Woodruffe in Surrey.

The blue and mauve borders at Hursley Park were part of a whole series of special colour schemes for the kitchen garden. Jekyll admitted herself that this was a particularly difficult colour combination: 'The cooler colours, blue and mauve and all the many shades of purple, require rather special arrangement for the forming of satisfactory garden pictures' (*A Gardener's Testament*). The borders ran on either side of a long grass walk which led to the grand herbaceous border I have already described (see page 24). Part of its planting is visible at the end of the walk and the flowers planted here are blue, pale yellow and white so that the cool, restful effect of the blue and mauve borders is not upset by hot flower colours.

My painting shows the planting scheme in August. I cannot be precise about the colours of two of the dahlias used in these borders so I have portrayed their colours according to their names and their relationship to other blooms in the planting scheme. The prominent border in the painting starts with a liberal planting of *Stachys olympica* in close association with ageratum, *Lavatera trimestris*, *Dahlia* 'Pink Star' and a gladiolus which Jekyll names 'America'. I believe that this was her own name for a gladiolus which was 'the much-prized gift of an American garden-loving friend' and she describes it as 'a beautiful Gladiolus of pale, cool pink colour' (*Colour in the Flower Garden*). The gladioli are followed by double *Malva moschata* with tall echinops and pink hollyhocks at the back of the border. *Clematis jackmanii* are planted behind the echinops in order to twine and flower among them once the echinops has finished flowering. White China asters (*Callistephus chinensis*) are planted at the front of the border to provide a foil to deep purple China asters further down the border. These in turn make an exciting contrast with the silvery foliage of *Artemisia ludoviciana* and the blue-grey foliage and steely blue flower heads of echinops standing behind. Godetia, stachys, blue China asters, larkspurs (*Delphinium consolida*) and *Limonium latifolia* continue the theme of restrained, cool colours and the first of these borders ends with white snapdragons and yet more deep purple China asters. At this point a grass path cuts between the first and second borders but, from the view-point I have taken, the path is not visible and the eye is led on to the next border, where the blue and mauve scheme is continued with a repeat of many of the plants already mentioned. These borders are backed by fruit trees.

The two borders opposite are backed and intersected by yew hedging which disguises a hard tennis court beyond. Only part of the first border can be seen in the picture and it begins with *Dahlia* 'Amethyst' followed by echinops and *Lavatera trimestris* with its pink flower cups standing out against the deep green of the yew hedge. *Gladiolus* 'America' is repeated in this border and is contrasted with the snapdragon 'Mauve Queen', deep purple China asters and *Salvia* 'Superba'. A planting of two varieties of scabious can just be glimpsed in this border at the forefront of the painting. The border beyond the bulge of the yew hedge continues with a repeat of most of the plants in the other borders.

The second garden I have chosen to paint is a delightful sunken garden, one of Jekyll's designs for the grounds of a large Edwardian house sited high above the Hampden Valley, near Great Missenden. Rignall Wood was built in 1909 by the architects Adams & Holden for Sir Felix Semon, a distinguished physician whose patients included the Kaiser, Queen Victoria and her son Edward VII. After Sir Felix Semon, the house had several owners and was used as a gathering place for the Free French during the last war; Charles de Gaulle was known to have been a visitor. H. Percy Adams had already worked with Jekyll on the King Edward VII Sanatorium at Midhurst where she had designed the gardens.

The design of the grounds at Rignall Wood must have presented problems to Jekyll because of the steepness of the site and, in common with other parts of the Chilterns, there is only a shallow layer of top soil over chalk. Letters from the architects to Jekyll record the problems of landscaping the site; vast quantities of soil had to be removed: 'The only thing that I can see we can possibly do is to take off some of the Bank say 500 loads and put it on the garden at A.A [plan reference] this will cost £45. Do you think we are justified in doing this at such an *extra* expense or shall we let the garden remain as it is and ease off the Bank of lawn a little. These Banks don't look well as they are nearly all chalk'. There are several changes of level and this involved elaborate terracing. When I visited Rignall Wood I was amazed that Jekyll was able to produce such a successful series of plans, twenty-seven of which are still in existence today, without having visited the site.

The garden today still has immense charm, and any planting by its present owners has been sensitively considered so that the original character of the Jekyll garden is preserved. At the front of the house, a flight of steps leads up to a wild garden which is still carpeted with primroses, violets and daffodils in the spring. Many of the trees here are believed to be original including a fine old medlar. Behind the house and overlooking the valley, the gardens are arranged in a series of terraces. On the level just below the building, the site of Jekyll's rose garden, there is now a discreet stone-edged swimming pool. Steps lead down to the next level of the garden where a handsome pergola shades a long walk and, from here, the level drops again to a generous lawn once used for croquet or bowling.

The sunken garden which was so intricately planted out by Jekyll on paper may never have been implemented. The site with its stone steps appears exactly as it does on Jekyll's plan but a rill garden has been constructed here instead of the rectangular borders proposed by Jekyll. Today the elegance of the site has been marred by having this garden divided in two. One half of the watercourse runs under a fence into the garden of the lodge next door.

In the architect's drawing the sunken garden had a simple formal design with two rectangular borders centrally placed in a large rectangular recessed area surrounded by shallow terraced walls. I have shown this as a paved garden, but it is possible that the site may have been grassed. The layout was typical of many sunken gardens of the period. Here Jekyll was not producing a planting scheme within the elaborate and often intrusive array of cleverly designed stonework conceived by Sir Edwin Lutyens; any originality or character in the garden's design depended on her planting.

The colour scheme which Jekyll created was one of purple-blues, blue-greys, lilac-pinks and creamy whites with a predominance of soft-textured grey foliage to set the flower colours off to advantage. She added pale yellow verbascum to complement the blues. The whole effect, which I have tried to capture in my painting, is rich and subtle with the kind of harmonious blend of colours one finds in a carefully worked tapestry.

My painting concentrates on one half of the sunken garden, imagined as it would have appeared in early June, and I have taken an angled view of the site so that a large section of the planting can be seen. A focus in the centre of the rectangular border is *Magnolia stellata* flanked on either side by tall violet blue *Delphinium consolida*. Jekyll does not specify this variety on her plan, but I believe she would have chosen this favourite annual larkspur as it fitted into her colour scheme. The verbascum planted on either side of the larkspurs was her favourite *Verbascum olympicum* with its 'towering candelabrum of pale yellow' and velvet-textured grey foliage; a perfect foil for the adjacent blue of the larkspurs. The pink rose 'Zéphirine Drouhin' is planted at either end of the border. Groups of peonies also feature in the border and I have illustrated the single-flowered *Paeonia lactiflora* in shades of deep pink and creamy white. *Delphinium grandiflora*, polemonium and *Anchusa azurea* 'Opal' add their different shades of blue to the scheme. The border is fringed with generous drifts of pink and white pinks and soft grey stachys.

Pinks are repeated again as edging to the far border in my painting, where dicentra, eryngium and campanula combine with iris varieties to produce a rich texture of plants. Jekyll used a selection of irises, with their distinctive blooms and sword-like leaves, to provide focal points among the other plants. The irises were arranged to punctuate this border at carefully chosen intervals. Jekyll's method of planting them among other plants to add interest and structure to a border was common to many of her gardens and it is obvious that the iris was one of her favourite plants. On occasion she planned terraced gardens predominantly of irises (see Chapter Eight, Walsham House, page 93), and specialised borders combining irises with other plants, as shown in her book *Colour*

XI. Hursley Park Blue and Mauve Borders

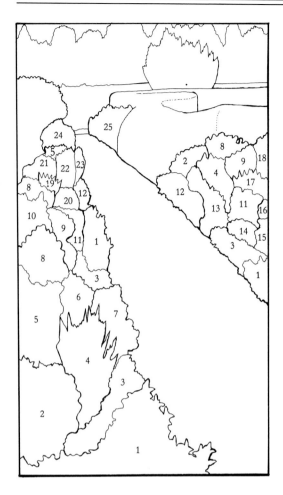

16. *Scabiosa* 'Azure Fairy' (*S. atropurpurea* 'Azure Fairy').
17. *Salvia virgata (S. virgata nemorosa* [syn. *S. × superba*]).
18. *Dahlia* 'Amethyst', lilac small-flowered cactus dahlia.
19. Iris = tall bearded iris – 'Kharput'.
20. Double rose godetia sown in border.
21. White dahlia.
22. Purple *Delphinium consolida* – larkspur, sown in border.
23. *Statice latifolia (Limonium latifolia).*
24. Continuation of right-hand border with plants already listed and drifts of: erigeron, white *Anemone japonica*, anchusa, delphiniums, lobelia, *Agathea coelestis (Felicia amelloides), Ageratum mexicanum* (syn. *A. houstonianum),* megasea (bergenia), *Campanula carpatica* and white snapdragons.
25. Continuation of left-hand border with plants already listed and drifts of: tradescantia = *Tradescantia × andersoniana, Plumbago larpentae (Ceratostigma plumbaginoides),* commelina = *Commelina coelestis, Gladiolus* 'Baron Hulot', deep violet purple [* 'Fidelio': ◊ 'Canterbury'].

Hursley Park Blue and Mauve Borders (page 39)

1. Stachys = *Stachys olympica* (syn. *S. byzantina*).
2. *Lavatera trimestris* sown in border.
3. Dwarf ageratum = *Ageratum houstonianum.*
4. *Gladiolus* 'America', cool pink [* 'Praha': ◊ 'Dreaming Spires Pink']
5. *Dahlia* 'Pink Star' [dahlia type untraced].
6. Double *Malva moschata.*
7. China aster 'Victoria White'.
8. Echinops = *Echinops ritro.*
9. *Artemisia ludoviciana.*
10. Pink hollyhock 'Palling Belle'.
11. Deepest purple China aster.
12. China aster 'Victoria Blue'.
13. Snapdragon 'Mauve Queen'.
14. *Gnaphalium luteoalbum* [choose silver-leaved foliage plant].
15. *Scabiosa caucasica.*

in the Flower Garden where irises and lupins are planted together to create an interesting blend of plant shapes and colours.

The tall bearded irises which Jekyll suggested for the sunken garden at Rignall Wood were a typical choice. Two blue bicolours 'Nationale' and 'Poiteau', and a blue self-coloured hybrid 'Sultane' contribute to the blue theme of flower colours in the garden. The Spanish iris 'L'Unique' adds a fresh combination of violet blue standards and white falls decorated with a golden-yellow marking.

The genetic structure of Jekyll's irises was based on two sets of genes (diploid) whereas today's hybrids have been bred with four sets of genes (tetraploid) so that irises currently grown in Britain and America have more substantial flowers with stronger stems to support them. But a more noticeable difference is in the choice of colours. Modern tall bearded irises come in a wide range of tones and blends which are brighter and cleaner than the colours of hybrids available to Jekyll. Nevertheless, the irises chosen for Rignall Wood make an important contribution to the prevailing colour scheme of the sunken garden.

Overhanging the far border from the terrace above are the roses 'Mme. Plantier' and 'Blush Damask', with their mass of white and pale pink blooms. Pink China roses are a predominant feature of the border in the foreground mixed with lavender and rosemary, one of Jekyll's most familiar combinations of plants. White, pale pink and yellow snapdragons, not shown in bloom in my painting, would have extended the flowering season of the garden when earlier plants were no longer in flower.

Jekyll is so often associated with soft pastel colour schemes but the next garden shows that she was equally skilful in her use of strong vibrant colours. The garden of Little Cumbrae, situated on an isolated island in the Firth of Clyde, has an ostentatious scheme of red and gold.

Little Cumbrae is a small privately owned island situated about a twenty-minute boat journey from the larger island of Great Cumbrae. When I visited the island it was on a day following gales and the journey across to the island, bobbing up and down in a small fishing boat on a rough sea, seemed longer but made me appreciate my arrival on dry land all the more. The first prominent feature of the island which I noticed from the sea was an old castle keep, standing on a jutting promontory of land that becomes a small separate island at high tide. The keep was built as a watch post against Nordic invaders, but later became a royal residence of Robert II of Scotland. Cromwell's troops tried to burn it down in 1653 and the erosion of sea winds have taken their toll. Today it is a romantic looking ruin and a nesting place for flocks of pigeons which, I later discovered, provide the present gardens with an invaluable source of manure from their droppings.

Sea birds covered the rocks close to the island. But my attention was caught by the drifts of daffodils, planted by the present owner of Little Cumbrae on the grass-covered shelves of rock that form natural terraces on the island. The old stone house, once an inn used by the crews of sailing ships awaiting customs clearance, stands on a flat area of land surrounded by its gardens and it appeared exactly as I had imagined it from the architects' original drawings.

XII. Rignall Wood Sunken Garden

The painting shows one half of this sunken garden designed for Rignall Wood in the Chilterns, a property once owned by Queen Victoria's physician. The colour scheme was typical of Jekyll, a harmonious blend of purple-blues, grey, pink, white and pale yellow. Stone

steps lead down to the paved area surrounding a rectangular border which has at its centre *Magnolia stellata* flanked by blue delphiniums and pale yellow verbascum. The rose 'Zéphirine Drouhin' is planted at either end of the border. In the borders in the foreground of the painting China roses are planted among lavender and rosemary. In the background, roses overhang a border of mixed plants edged with pinks.

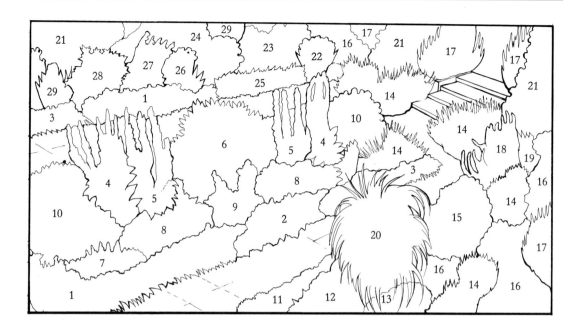

Rignall Wood Sunken Garden (pages 42–3)

1. Pink pinks.
2. Polemonium = *Polemonium caeruleum.*
3. White pinks.
4. Verbascum = *Verbascum olympicum.*
5. Delphinium.
6. *Magnolia stellata.*
7. *Delphinium grandiflorum.*
8. Peony = *Paeonia lactiflora* [Jekyll refers to this as *P. albiflora*].
9. *Anchusa* 'Opal' (*A. azurea* 'Opal').
10. Rose 'Zéphirine Drouhin'.
11. Cerastium.
12. *Cistus laurifolius.*
13. *Clematis recta.*
14. Lavender = *Lavandula angustifolia.*
15. Weigela = *Weigela florida.*
16. China rose = 'Old Blush'.
17. Rosemary.
18. Nepeta = *Nepeta* × *faassenii.*
19. Iris = tall bearded iris – 'Nationale', blue bicolour [* 'Amigo', 'Wabash', 'Braithwaite': ◊ 'Proud Tradition', 'Best Bet', 'Glistening Icicle', 'Nordic Seas', 'River Hawk'].
20. Eulalia *(Miscanthus sinensis).*
21. Rose 'Mme Plantier'.
22. Iris = tall bearded iris – 'Poiteau', blue bicolour [* 'Amigo', 'Wabash', 'Braithwaite': ◊ 'Proud Tradition', 'Best Bet', 'Glistening Icicle', 'Nordic Seas', 'River Hawk'].
23. *Anemone japonica.*
24. Rose 'Blush Gallica' ('Blush Damask').
25. Dicentra = *Dicentra eximia.*
26. Iris = Spanish iris – 'L' Unique', blue/white [*choose from many available in bulb catalogues: ◊ 'Wedgewood', 'Imperator'].
27. *Campanula macrantha (Campanula latifolia).*
28. *Eryngium* × *oliverianum.*
29. Iris = tall bearded iris – 'Sultane', blue self [* 'Jane Philips', 'Harbor Blue', Patterdale': ◊ 'Sapphire Hills', 'Tide's In', 'Song of Norway', 'Lake Placid', 'Carved Crystal', 'Olympiad', 'Victoria Falls'].

The gardens provided me with a surprise: here were terraced walls, paved pathways and curved landing steps fringed with aubretias that would have appeared perfectly at home in Surrey. These features bore the unmistakeable characteristics of so many of Jekyll's English gardens, but the use of local stone blended the hard landscaping into its natural surroundings.

The original garden layout has been well maintained and the planting, although not Jekyll's, has been skilfully designed to enhance the charm of its stone walls and paths. The front garden is laid out in double terraces with a dense green lawn reaching down to the sea wall; but the area allocated for borders is less generous than appears on Jekyll's plan. A stone path leads into the paved garden which is the subject of my painting.

Jekyll had been commissioned to produce her ideas for the gardens through architects acting for a wealthy American, Evelyn W. Parker. Parker was an enthusiastic yachtsman, a member of a social set which included Edward VII, and his association with the Tate and Lyle family had enabled him to make his money through trade in sugar. His attraction to the island may have been its proximity to Largs on the Scottish mainland, which was a thriving yachting centre at this period. Parker's attachment to Little Cumbrae extended after his death for his ashes lie buried on the island.

The extensive work which was needed to convert the house into a comfortable home and to lay out the garden was carried out at the height of the First World War, and it was remarkable that a project of this kind could have been undertaken at this period. Even in peace time, the operation of transporting quantities of good top soil across the sea from the mainland would have been a difficult exercise involving a number of men. Jekyll's plans, nine of which including the architects' drawings still exist, were begun in 1916 but it was only in the following year that Parker wrote to her: 'I send you some snapshots of the Little Cumbrae, from which you may get some idea of the place but they are not very clear. The masonry is a milky grey color & the slates a greeny grey, on the other side I give you a sketch plan in order to localize the views. What fearful weather!'.

Jekyll's bold yet limited colour scheme for the little paved garden in my painting was a perfect choice for this setting. The grey stonework of the house and of the walls and paving used in this garden needed to be enlivened by strong, warm colours. The paved garden was planned with borders of annual plants in its centre and herbaceous plants surrounding the central paved area. At first, I wondered whether the annual planting plan was an example of one of Jekyll's temporary schemes designed to be used prior to permanent planting. The formal layout of borders would have been ideal for a rose garden and the present owner has used the site for this purpose for many years judging from the age of the roses planted there today. However, a different site altogether was marked out on Jekyll's plans as 'the rose garden', so one must assume that the annual scheme planned for the paved garden was designed to be repeated every summer.

Nevertheless, roses were planted as a central feature in this garden. A rose temple was designed to occupy a diamond-shaped area of grass at the centre of the annual borders. Although the temple is clearly marked on the drawings, I feel that the idea originated from either the architects or their client. I find it hard to believe that Jekyll would have approved of such an ornamental garden conceit, which was also potentially so precarious, for a windswept Scottish island. I have, however, for the sake of accurately

XIII. Little Cumbrae Red and Gold Paved Garden

A garden of predominantly annual plants designed to complement an old stone house on a
small island in the Firth of Clyde, Scotland, once owned by a wealthy American sugar trader.
The central focus of the garden is a rose temple surrounded by a geometric diamond-shaped

arrangement of beds planted with cannas, *Ricinus communis*, begonias and dahlias in rich warm colours. The far border in the painting, sheltered by the walls of the garden and a screen of tamarisk, is also planted with perennials – kniphofia, helenium and rudbeckia. In the background is a view of the Firth and the Scottish mainland and an old castle keep standing on a tidal island.

Little Cumbrae Red and Gold Garden (pages 46–7)

1. *Ricinus* 'Gibsonii (*Ricinus communis* 'Gibsonii').
2. Acanthus = *Acanthus mollis*.
3. Red canna.
4. Yellow begonia.
5. *Zea japonica variegata* = variegated *Zea mays*.
6. Yellow canna.
7. *Megasea cordifolia (Bergenia cordifolia).*
8. Variegated mint.
9. *Gladiolus* × *brenchleyensis*, tall/red flowers [* 'Oscar', 'Trader Horn': ◊ 'St. Peters'].
10. *Dahlia* 'Fire King'. Described as both a scarlet cactus or decorative dahlia. Also named 'Glare of the Garden'.
11. *Canna* 'Adrien Ruberini'? = canna with reddish foliage.
12. Primrose African marigolds.
13. *Dahlia* 'King of the Belgians' [untraceable]. 'King Leopold', pale yellow peony-flowered dahlia.
14. *Dahlia* 'Henry Patrick', described as both a white cactus and decorative dahlia.
15. *Dahlia* 'Cochineal', crimson-toned brown. Described as both a decorative and cactus dahlia.
16. *Dahlia* 'Victoria', single white dahlia with crimson-margined petals.
17. White begonia.
18. Red begonia.
19. *Gladiolus* 'Lily Lehman', pale sulphur yellow, rose flakings [* 'Spic and Span': ◊ 'King's College'].
20. Vine = vitis.
21. Rose temple.
22. Hydrangea.
23. *Pyrethrum uliginosum (Leucanthemella serotina).*
24. *Aster corymbosis (A. divaricatus).*
25. Leycesteria = *Leycesteria formosa*.
26. Dwarf French marigolds.
27. *Helenium pumilum.*
28. Tritoma (Kniphofia).
29. Orange African marigolds.
30. *Helenium striatum (H. autumnale striatum*, gold and crimson [*H. hoopesii* 'Red and Gold': ◊ *H. autumnale* 'Gartensonne'].
31. *Rudbeckia speciosa (R. fulgida speciosa).*
32. Tamarisk = *Tamarix pentandra* (Jekyll also used *T. gallica* for hedging).
33. *Sedum telephium.*

reflecting the plan shown the temple, but without the raised 'altar' which was sometimes placed at the centre of these structures. Jekyll did not specify the roses for the temple so I have only indicated foliage.

The four beds surrounding the central diamond were, in Jekyll's own words, to be 'treated alike and symmetrically. The middle and outer portions are in strong, warm colouring, the inner sides in white & yellow'. She describes the plants chosen to achieve this effect: 'Ricinus Gibsonii & Canna 'Adrien Ruberi' [?] have reddish foliage. Sedum Telephium is a fine garden form of the native plant with broad heads of chocolate red blooms in September. Var. mint is the variegated form of Mentha rotundifolia. It should not be allowed to flower & be kept pinched back to not more than 10″ high. The megasea is M. cordifolia. The bloom which comes early in the year should be cut out to throw all the strength into the handsome foliage. The maize is the kind striped with white, Zea japonica variegata'.

The centre of the borders is planted out with groups of dahlias: 'Henry Patrick', a pure white cactus dahlia, in the centre flanked by a dahlia which Jekyll refers to as 'King of the Belgians'. I have not been able to trace this variety and I wonder if she could have meant this to be 'King Leopold', a pale clear yellow paeony-flowered dahlia, as this would have fitted into the colour scheme. The reds are represented by 'Cochineal', a decorative dahlia which a contemporary catalogue describes as 'crimson toned with brown' and Jekyll's favourite 'Fire King' which she rates as 'among the most gorgeous of our September flowers'. A white single dahlia with crimson margined petals, 'Victoria', is her final choice. The dahlias are surrounded with bold groups of red and yellow canna and the coppery-leafed *Ricinus communis* 'Gibsonii'. Red, yellow and white begonias punctuated by groups of bergenia and variegated mint edge the borders and acanthus give form and emphasis to the corners of the four borders. Primrose African marigolds are ranged in a generous drift behind the yellow begonias. Two old varieties of autumn flowering gladioli are used to extend the flowering season; *Gladiolus* x *brenchleyensis*, a brilliant scarlet variety producing blooms on handsome erect spikes, and G. 'Lily Lehmann', with pale sulpur yellow blooms which fade to cream and rose. These would not have been in flower in early September, the time at which my painting illustrates the garden.

Just glimpsed through the arches of the rose temple is a small circle of grass which was the site for a sundial. This is surrounded with lavender, hydrangeas and myrtle. The herbaceous borders surrounding the formal paved garden continue the warm colour scheme with marigolds, helenium and rudbeckia and a repeat of *Ricinus communis* 'Gibsonii'. Kniphofia adds a bold architectural effect. The present owner told me that he had taken out masses of these plants, perhaps self-sown from Jekyll's day, as they had taken over the borders and became untidy due to wind damage. There is no evidence today of the tamarisk hedge which Jekyll had suggested to give some protection to the garden.

I have chosen the final garden in this chapter not only for its refined and delicate colour scheme but also because it is an example of Jekyll's planting design for a child's garden. This garden featured on one of the original plans for Woodruffe, a one and a half acre garden in Surrey, produced by Jekyll in 1909 for her client, Mrs. Johnstone. Nine of

XIV. Woodruffe Child's Garden

Soft colours and cottage garden favourites were chosen by Jekyll for this child's garden in Surrey. Many of these plants were also recommended in *Children and Gardens.*

these plans exist today and study of them confirms that the present garden still retains its original Jekyll layout with the exception of the pergola which was resited. The gardens include a paved garden with decoratively shaped beds, long double borders divided by a path and set between thick hedges, an immaculate tennis lawn and the fine pergola. The site of the child's garden has now been grassed over but the arches behind the site, which are a continuation of the pergola, are still in good condition.

Jekyll must have presented a rather forbidding figure to children. Although she had come from a family of four boys and an elder sister, she spent much of her youth as a solitary child; her brothers were away at school and her sister was seven years her senior. So, as an adult, she was impatient with the unpredictability, untidiness and, particularly, the noise of childhood. However, in 1908, she produced a delightful book, *Children and Gardens*, in which she showed that she could recall her own enthusiasm for gardens as a child and share this remembered experience sympathetically with her young readers.

As a child, she and her sister Carrie were given two adjacent plots: 'Great was my pride and delight when I was first given a garden of my own'. Among the plants which she grew in this little plot were many that she later included in *Children and Gardens* in the chapter 'Flowers For Your Own Garden'. She followed much of her own advice about the choice of plants when she came to design the child's garden at Woodruffe.

My painting shows a corner of this garden in June. In the background are the stone piers of the pergola with their wooden arches and, through these, one can see shrubs and woodland. The colour scheme in this corner of the garden is a mixture of pinks enhanced by white and touches of blue. There is an edging of London Pride (*Saxifraga* x *urbium*), blue aubrieta and white pinks. On the left of my painting is the thornless rose, 'Zéphirine Drouhin', followed by groups of monarda and valerian and the miniature pompon rose, 'Mignonette' ('Cécile Brunner'). A mat of cerastium with its tiny white flowers and soft grey leaves separates 'Mignonette' from a damask rose and I have painted 'Blush Damask'. The spikes of iris leaves contrast with the softer informal habit of the other plants. White snapdragons and *Campanula persicifolia* can be seen behind 'Zéphirine Drouhin' and a matching group of snapdragons is on the right of the picture next to a clump of tall pink lupins. The garden is backed by weigela punctuated by groups of sweet peas which would have twined among their branches, covering these shrubs in a mass of sweetly scented blooms.

Chapter Four

Seasonal Borders

THE THREE GARDENS in this chapter are all examples of Jekyll's ability to plan for all-the-year-round or particular seasonal interest. The first garden, Chart Cottage in Kent, is a modest sized cottage garden with an attractive feature of shrub borders planted on either side of a long stretch of lawn. In this garden Jekyll planned a seasonal sequence of flowering and fruiting shrubs, starting in the spring and continuing into autumn with a fine display of berries. There was even to be winter interest provided by a number of evergreens.

The early spring garden at Marksdanes in Somerset is a good example of the type of specialised seasonal planting which Jekyll designed for many of her clients. The prototype of this spring display of plants was Jekyll's own garden at Munstead Wood where a pathway runs between borders carpeted with drifts of early spring flowers. Marksdanes had many of Jekyll's favourites: primroses, hellebores, omphalodes and forget-me-nots. Rows of cob-nuts, underplanted with ferns, enclosed and gave protection to the garden.

The 'old fashioned English garden', as it was described by Jekyll's American client, was designed to complement the old historic Glebe House in Woodbury, Connecticut. This garden was predominantly intended for a summer show of cottage garden flowers ranging from soft pinks and blues to bright yellow, orange and red with tall white lilies to give a distinctive touch of elegance, typical of Jekyll.

Chart Cottage represents most people's idea of a charming period country cottage but is, in fact, an amalgam of three small adjoining cottages dating from 1350 to 1750. The building which has an attractive half-tiled brick and stone frontage sits slightly off-centre on its site, with a good sized lawn at the front and gardens at the side and back of the building. There are six plans remaining of Jekyll's original scheme and they illustrate her ability to handle the design of a relatively small site of one and a half acres.

Jekyll was commissioned to plan the garden in 1911 for Bernard Blunt who, in his letters to Jekyll, describes himself as 'a very keen gardener' who had 'struggled for the last twelve years in the north of Finland within 100 miles of the Arctic Circle where one has three months summer and nine months snow and ice, I have therefore had very little experience of English gardening'. He expressed a preference for 'some Lilies and Hibiscus shrubs, both of which I am very fond of, and like everyone else I love Roses and Sweet Peas'.

Jekyll's plans combined many features. The front garden was set out in a complex series of beds lavishly planted with a variety of flowering plants. Yew-hedged bowers, which still exist in good condition, sheltered seats from where the display of blooms could be enjoyed. On one side of the house there were the shrub borders that I feature in my painting and a small rose garden still enclosed by its original yew hedging. Behind the cottage, there were more shrubs and trees and a kitchen garden.

The present owners of Chart Cottage have an ambitious scheme to restore the garden to its original state and planting. They have begun with the little formal rose garden, acquiring the original varieties of roses from sources in Britain and America. Of the original Jekyll planting little remains except for a few pines, the stump of a birch, some rhododendrons and a 'red cedar' marked on Jekyll's plan.

The shrub borders which I have painted were planned to occupy either side of a long stretch of lawn which ended in a formal feature of octagonal paving. The design for this garden is similar to the layout of the Hill Top herbaceous borders described on page 25; it gives a sense of space and elegance to what, in many other respects, is just a generous sized cottage garden. Although I have shown the borders in late May, this garden was designed for all-the-year-round interest. There are a number of evergreens so that the borders would still have leafage in winter and the generous plantings of skimmia and *Viburnum opulus* would have ensured a rich crop of berries in the autumn. A long narrow lawn cuts between the borders and leads to an octagonal paved area backed by yew hedging. The three-sided stone seat here provides a viewpoint for the garden. This is a slightly sloping site with the border and grass path on the right of the picture being higher than the left-hand side. The view from the seat would have led up to the rose garden, enclosed by a yew hedge. The path on the right, possibly because of water draining to this lower level of the site, was surfaced in some way. I have shown it gravelled.

The shrubs used in these borders are azaleas; these were Ghent and Knap Hill hybrids including some unusual old varieties. In the left-hand border in my painting, Jekyll uses a favourite combination of azaleas: 'Of these the first is the pale yellow double *narcissiflora*, then another well-known kind named Nancy Waterer, a large flower of a full soft yellow;... leading to the glorious deep orange Gloria Mundi' (*A Gardener's Testament*). Behind this group is an old variety of azalea, *Azalea viscosepalum*, a tall erect Ghent hybrid with small pale cream fragrant flowers. Jekyll achieved the most exciting effects by using gradations in tone of the same colour, in this case soft cream and pale golden yellows and then a wonderful burnt orange. In the right-hand border, Jekyll turns from gold to pinks with an azalea which Jekyll refers to as *Azalea incana* which I believe to be *Azalea incanatum* 'Floribundum', another old variety with rosy salmon flowers. It is planted near to Azalea 'Fama': 'The splendid old Fama, a full rosy pink, always smothered with bloom' (*A Gardener's Testament*).

Evergreens like rosemary, skimmia and *Rhododendron myrtifolium* are used at the front of the borders. It is interesting that Jekyll, in this garden, mixed rhododendrons and azaleas, a feature she usually advocated against: 'Azaleas should never be planted among or even within sight of Rhododendrons' (*Wood and Garden*). She listed only three main varieties of rhododendron for Chart Cottage. These are, for the outer borders, *Rhododendron ponticum* and *Rhododendron multimaculatum*, an old variety which Jekyll claims 'has the best foliage of all; it is much to be regretted that it is now despised by growers, because the individual blooms are narrow petalled. But indoors, as a cut flower, it has, just for this reason, a distinction and charming refinement that make it

XV. Chart Cottage Seasonal Shrub Borders

The formal layout for these shrub borders, which Jekyll designed in 1911 for a cottage garden in Kent, was similar to the design she used for Hill Top's herbaceous borders (pages 26/27). At Chart Cottage, the shrub borders and long narrow lawn lead the eye to an octagonal area

of paving, sheltered by hedging, with a stone seat from which to view the garden. The shrubs were chosen to give all-the-year-round interest. The painting shows the garden in late May with rhododendrons, azaleas, cistus, olearias and peonies in flower. Evergreen trees – conifers and hollies – provide a dark background for the flowering shrubs and blossoming trees.

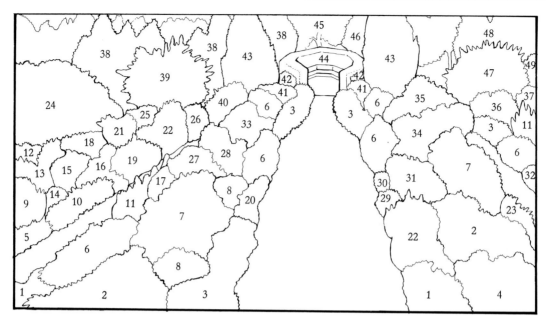

Chart Cottage Seasonal Shrub Borders
(pages 54–5)

1. *Artemisia arborescens.*
2. *Cistus laurifolius.*
3. Skimmia = *Skimmia japonica.*
4. Tree peonies = *Paeonia suffruticosa.*
5. *Rudbeckia speciosa (R. fulgida speciosa).*
6. *Rhododendron myrtifolium.*
7. Water Elder = *Viburnum opulus.*
8. *Veronica traversii (Hebe brachysiphon).*
9. Tall bearded iris 'Purple King', red/purple self [* 'Matinata', 'Royal Touch', 'Sable Night': ◊ 'Midnight Hour', 'Titan's Glory', 'Master Touch', 'Loyalist', 'Persian Gown', 'Royal Satin'].
10. Stachys = *Stachys olympica (syn. S. byzantina).*
11. *Olearia gunniana (O. phlogopappa).*
12. Helenium = *Helenium autumnale.*
13. Tritoma (Kniphofia).
14. Monarda = *Monarda didyma.*
15. Iris = Spanish iris – 'L'Unique', blue/white [*Choose from many available in bulb catalogues: ◊ 'Wedgewood', 'Imperator'].
16. *Geranium grandiflorum (G. himalayense).*
17. *Rhus cotinus (Cotinus coggygria).*
18. *Chrysanthemum maximum.*
19. Santolina = *Santolina chamaecyparissus.*
20. *Megasea cordifolia (Bergenia cordifolia).*
21. Tall bearded iris 'Sultane', blue self [* 'Jane Philips', 'Harbor Blue', 'Patterdale': ◊ 'Sapphire Hills', 'Tide's In', 'Song of Norway', 'Lake Placid', 'Carved Crystal', 'Olympiad', 'Victoria Falls'].
22. Rosemary.
23. Cotoneaster.
24. *Rhododendron ponticum.*
25. *Iris orientalis (syn. I. ochroleuca).*
26. Lavender = *Lavandula angustifolia*
27. *Azalea* 'Gloria Mundi', deep orange [* 'Coccinea speciosa', 'Sulley': ◊ 'Copper Cloud' (Ilams): 'Gibralter' (Knap Hill)].
28. *Azalea* 'Nancy Waterer'.
29. Centranthus = *Centranthus ruber.*
30. *Veronica filifolia.*
31. Stephanandra = *Stephanandra incisa.*
32. Verbena.
33. *Azalea* 'Narcissiflora'.
34. *Azalea incana = A. incanatum floribundum,* rosy salmon [* 'Josephine Klinger', 'Freya', 'Bouquet des Flore', 'Cecile', 'Homebush', 'Strawberry Ice': ◊ 'Peachy Keen' (Ilams), 'Pink Williams' (Ilams)].
35. *Azalea* 'Fama', rose pink [* 'Raphael de Smet': ◊ 'Flamingo', 'Sylphides', both Knap Hill].
36. White broom = *Cytisus albus.*
37. Golden elder = *Sambucus nigra aurea.*
38. Holly = Ilex.
39. *Pyrus malus floribunda [Malus floribunda].*
40. *Azalea* 'Viscosepalum'.
41. *Kalmia latifolia.*
42. *Rhododendron ferrugineum.*
43. Red cedar = *Thuja plicata.*
44. Yew = Taxus.
45. Existing apple tree i.e. predating Jekyll's plan.
46. Bay = *Laurus nobilis.*
47. White thorn = *Crataegus monogyna.*
48. Cypress = Cupressus.
49. *Rhododendron multimaculatum,* milk-white flowers, rose-red blotch [* 'Sappho'].

much better for this use than the greater number of the massive blooms that alone satisfy the florist. It is white – the soft, cool white of skim-milk, and the blotch is a cluster of spots of a very beautiful rosy red' (*A Gardener's Testament*). The inner borders have an edging of *Rhododendron myrtifolium* and there is also a discreet planting of Jekyll's favourite Alpenrose, *Rhododendron ferrugineum*.

Other shrubs include *Viburnum opulus*: 'The Water-elder now makes a brave show... It is without doubt the most beautiful berry-bearing shrub of mid-September. The fruit hangs in ample clusters from the point of every branch and of every lateral twig, in colour like the brightest of red currants, but with a translucent lustre that gives each separate berry a much brighter look; the whole bush shows fine warm colouring, the leaves having turned to a rich red... It is the parent of the well-known Guelder-Rose, which is merely its double-flowered form' (*Wood and Garden*).

Cistus laurifolius is also planted in generous groups in both borders. Among these main groups of shrubs are *Hebe brachysiphon*, *Olearia phlogopappa*, *Cotinus coggygria*, stephanandra and two tall sentinels of red cedar. *Malus floribunda* and a white cratageus echo the blossom of the apple orchard which can just be seen in the background of the painting.

The planting plans for Marksdanes in Somerset, fourteen of which exist today, were produced by Jekyll in 1919. The house had been built in 1845 on a field which appears on old local tithe maps and gave the house its name. Jekyll worked through an architect, A.J. Pictor, but a great deal of information was provided by her client, Mrs. Hester Torrance.

The letters from Mrs. Torrance are a good example of the nightmare Jekyll must have encountered many times over, working on plans of gardens that she never visited and with a nervous client who had to be dealt with at long distance. Mrs. Torrance writes:

I don't quite know how it is, but the Yews have got a little wrong as to position, the Yew in C.1. [plan reference] should really be where the Birch C.2. is & the Birch is still more behind, but as it turns out to be dead it does not matter, so the square of Yew which the path ends in, is right up against the Irish Yew. Your suggestion of K.4. as a place for meals is very good, but unfortunately there is no shade, & since you suggested it, I have sat there, & it is too noisy, you might as well be in the kitchen... I am afraid it is quite impossible to have the maids garden where you suggest, as the addition to the house there is a coal cellar, & they do not put the coal in bags here, but like to get the cart close to the cellar door & shovel it in, also we must have some place for a motor or carriage to turn in, if it was a wet day & some one was coming to see me, I could <u>not</u> expect them to talk [walk?] all the way from the gate, & then a cab with luggage where would it turn, so we must keep that space clear, also another reason, there are some man holes there, & it would not do to cover them up, in case we wanted to inspect the drains. I am afraid the Winter Garden is much under the trees, nothing would ever do there, they are big trees, & their branches came right over the path, also M.1. is just nothing but roots; so please suggest another Winter Garden. My husband has just said he thinks you intend cabs etc to turn in the stable yard, but anyhow that does not get over the difficulty of the coal cellar.

It is perhaps hardly surprising that little is apparent today of Jekyll's planting schemes for Marksdanes and one wonders whether Mrs. Torrance lost heart in the face of all the difficulties she records in her letters and never implemented any of Jekyll's plans for the garden.

I have painted the 'Nutwalk and Spring Garden' in late March. The planting scheme is typical of Jekyll with generous drifts of spring-flowering plants interweaving with each other. Behind these are two rows of Cob-nuts (*Corylus avellana*) underplanted with male ferns (*Dryopteris filix-mas*), not yet showing at this time of year. A walk, which I have imagined to be grass, leads in between the rows of nuts and ends at a yew-sheltered alcove with a seat. Jekyll had originally planned this as a June garden but her notes indicate that this was to be changed to 'March, April, May – not June', and that the garden should have 'Nuts with Primroses, Lent Hellebores'. The present owners of the house can find no sign of this garden apart from a profusion of daffodils in spring, but these were never indicated on Jekyll's plan.

The walk is defined at either end with clumps of bergenia followed, on the left-hand side of the picture, by drifts of Solomon's Seal, aquilegia, *Omphalodes verna*, primroses, myosotis, uvularia – 'The graceful North American *Uvularia grandiflora*, in habit like a small Solomon's Seal' (*Colour in the Flower Garden*) – followed by further drifts of myosotis, primroses, Solomon's Seal and dentaria. Dentaria are now included with the cardamines and Jekyll may have used either the native *Cardamine bulbifera* or *Cardamine heptaphylla* which she refers to as '*Dentaria pinnata*, a woodland plant of Switzerland and Austria. . . one of the handsomest of the white flowered *cruciferae*' (*Wood and Garden*). The right-hand side of the path has a repeat of most of these plants but also includes clumps of Lenten hellebores (*Helleborus orientalis*) and epimedium. The nuts are shown barely in leaf but later in the year they would have indeed been 'a shady path of Filberts or Cobnuts arching overhead and yielding a bountiful autumn harvest' (*Colour in the Flower Garden*).

The Glebe House in Woodbury, Connecticut is a delightful old clapboard building, parts of which date from 1690, with a traditional New England cedar 'shake' gambrel roof and salt-box profile. Apart from its architectural value, it has an historical significance as the birthplace of the American Episcopal Church. On 25 March 1783, a few weeks after American Independence was secured, fourteen Anglican clergymen met in secret at the Glebe House, then the home of John Rutgers Marshall, the first Episcopal minister of Woodbury, and elected Samuel Seabury as their first bishop.

In 1923 a committee was formed to restore the Glebe House. The building was opened to the public in 1925 and the Seabury Society for the Preservation of the Glebe House was formed to ensure that the building would never again fall into a state of dilapidation. Miss Annie Burr Jennings, the daughter of a founder of Standard Oil, was an early member of the Society. She was a woman who gave generously to good causes and her own large garden surrounding her house was open throughout the summer months, without charge, to the public.

In 1926 Miss Jennings travelled to England with her brother and his wife and, during the course of her visit, she spent an afternoon with Gertrude Jekyll, taking tea and admiring the gardens at Munstead Wood. On returning to America she wrote an

XVI. Marksdanes Spring Borders

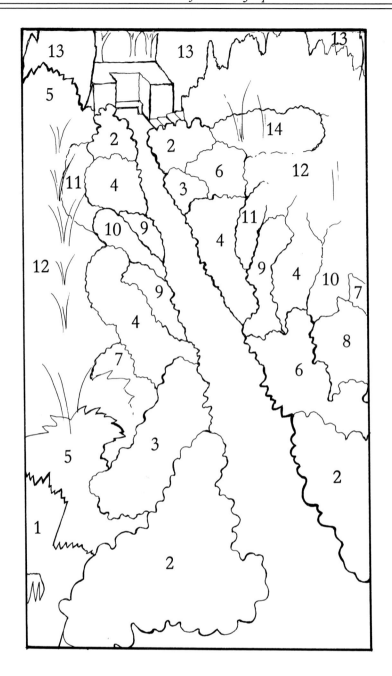

Marksdanes Spring Borders (page 59)

1. *Iris foetidissima.*
2. Megasea (Bergenia = *B. cordifolia*).
3. Omphalodes = *Omphalodes verna.*
4. Primrose = *Primula vulgaris.*
5. Solomon's Seal = *Polygonatum* × *hybridum.*
6. Lenten hellebore = *Helleborus orientalis.*
7. Aquilegia.
8. Epimedium = *Epimedium pinnatum.*
9. Myosotis = *Myosotis alpestris.*
10. Uvularia = *Uvularia grandiflora.*
11. Dentaria = *Dentaria pinnata (Cardamine heptaphylla).*
12. Cob-nuts = *Corylus avellana* underplanted with male fern *(Dryopteris filix-mas).*
13. Yew = Taxus.
14 *Rhododendron myrtifolium.*

enthusiastic letter to Jekyll: 'As soon as I returned I took up this matter of the Glebe House. . . it has been agreed by the committee that we should have an old fashioned garden there. I am sending you a plan of the Glebe House, and also some extracts from newspapers. These extracts give a photograph of the house and I am sending you also measurements of the land. You can take your time in making a plan for an old fashioned garden for this Glebe House and I have permission to go ahead with arrangements, and I, personally, shall be responsible for the expense of these details. So kindly send me your bill when you have completed the work'. Her impetuosity had not taken account of the fact that the garden's design had already been undertaken by Miss Amy Cogswell of Norwich, Connecticut and the plants had already been ordered and planted. One forms the impression that Miss Jennings was a woman used to getting her own way because she was able to convince the Seabury Society, that, regardless of any previous commitment to Miss Cogswell and expense incurred, Jekyll should be commissioned to re-design the garden.

The plans which were sent to Jekyll included the newly designed areas and Jekyll commented favourably on some of Amy Cogswell's work: 'The little paved garden A to the South. It looks nicely done. . . does it want altering or renewing? The path B and border on each side. This also looks well planned'. Miss Jennings replied: 'The little paved garden <u>A</u> to the South. Yes, this needs renewing'. She was obviously keen that the garden would be re-designed by Jekyll regardless of any merits of the previous plan.

There is, however, no evidence remaining that Miss Jennings had her way. By October 1927, a local gardening club had reneged on their agreement to maintain the garden. Over the years it became neglected and so it is difficult to assess whether Jekyll's design was ever implemented. In the nineteen fifties a keen local gardener, Ethel Reinberg, attempted to save the garden from further ravages of time, and today an exciting project to plant out the Jekyll garden according to the original plans is under way. In 1987 the Jekyll at the Glebe House Committee was formed to raise funds 'to complete Miss Jekyll's garden as faithfully as possible according to her original conception'. With eight plans to work from, teams of volunteers, including many experts and students of horticulture, are presently involved in planting out the garden. In some cases, they may have to deviate from Jekyll's plan. As she herself admitted, she was not familiar with local conditions for growing plants: 'I have so little knowledge of actual planting over your side that I do not know if the evergreens I have shown will be the right ones, though your latitude is nearly the same as ours'. Problems are already indicated with her choice of China roses and rosemary, neither of which, according to one local newspaper report, would survive a Connecticut winter. But it is still too early to determine what deviations in planting will have to be made. At present, research still continues and meanwhile, traps have been put out to lure Japanese beetles, a pest with a voracious appetite for roses, away from the newly planted garden. The large old American sycamore or plane tree also poses problems because, although Jekyll when working on the plans for the Glebe House was concerned that it was diseased ('The large tree − Plane or Sycamore − seems to be dying or is already half dead − is there any thought of doing away with it?'), the tree has survived and now shades a large section of the garden in which Jekyll planned to have sun-loving plants.

XVII. The Glebe House Cottage Garden, Connecticut

An 'old-fashioned' garden, at present being restored, designed by Jekyll in 1926 to complement an historic house in Connecticut. The painting takes a high-level view of the garden so that its simple formal layout can be clearly seen. The borders were planned in a

colour sequence beginning, in the foreground of the picture, with cool colours, white blue and pink, and then building up to a vibrant display of warm colours, yellow, orange and red in the far border. Jekyll used many familiar cottage garden plants: hollyhocks, snapdragons, dahlias, the shasta daisy *Chrysanthemum maximum,* and the rayed flowers of helenium and rudbeckia. Tall white *Lilium candidum* punctuate the borders.

The Glebe House Cottage Garden
(pages 62–3)

1. Red cedar = *Thuja plicata.*
2. Lawson cypress = *Chamaecyparis lawsoniana.*
3. Portugal laurel = *Prunus lusitanica.*
4. Philadelphus.
5. Weigela [illegible].
6. Rosemary.
7. China rose.
8. Laurustinus *(Viburnum tinus).*
9. *Berberis aquifolium (Mahonia aquifolium).*
10. Existing lilac i.e. predating Jekyll's plan.
11. Existing plane or sycamore i.e. predating Jekyll's plan.
12. Funkia (hosta) = *Hosta sieboldiana.*
13. *Lilium candidum.*
14. White iris.
15. *Chrysanthemum maximum.*
16. Anchusa = *Anchusa azurea.*
17. White dahlia.
18. *Iris sibirica.*
19. *Veronica traversii (Hebe brachysiphon).*,
20. Pink snapdragons.
21. Megasea (bergenia = *Bergenia cordifolia).*
22. Peony = *Paeonia lactiflora* or *P. officinalis.*
23. White hollyhocks.
24. Tree ivy.
25. Lavender = *Lavandula angustifolia*
26. *Campanula macrantha (C. latifolia).*
27. Stachys = *Stachys olympica* (syn. *S. byzantina).*
28. *Geranium ibericum.*
29. *Ligustrum japonicum.*

30. *Spiraea lindleyana (Sorbaria lindleyana* [syn. *S. tomentosa]*).
31. Pink pinks.
32. Pink hollyhocks.
33. *Fuchsia gracilis (Fuchsia magellanica* 'Gracilis').
34. Centranthus = *Centranthus ruber.*
35. *Polygonum bunonsis (P. affine).*
36. Bronze iris.
37. *Helenium cupreum (H. autumnale cupreum,* wallflower colouring [* *H. hoopesii* 'Wyndley', 'Mahogany']).
38. Monarda = *Monarda didyma.*
39. Red dahlias.
40. Red hollyhocks.
41. *Oenothera fruticosa.*
42. *Rudbeckia speciosa (R. fulgida speciosa).*
43. *Helenium pumilum*
44. *Euonymous radicans variegata (E. fortunei* 'Variegata').
45. *Hemerocallis flava (H. lilio-asphodelus).*
46. Yellow iris.
47. White iris.
48. *Iberis sempervirens.*
49. Holly = *Ilex* 'Scotch Gold' [Choose golden variegated holly].

I have painted the garden in summer, shown as Jekyll probably imagined it — a profusion of bloom and colour with tall hollyhocks, so familiar in English cottage gardens, standing at the back of the herbaceous borders and elegant *Lilium candidum* puntuating the planting. The plants shown are those on her plan, without any allowance for changes in planting that the Jekyll at the Glebe House Committee may feel it is necessary to make to ensure complete hardiness and survival.

The plot is not a generous one and the house itself is quite small, so that an old fashioned cottage style of garden suits it admirably. The layout is simple and formal with a stone-flagged path leading up to the front door and a path going round one side of the house leading to a small paved rose garden which separates the main building from a power house situated behind it. In her plan Jekyll incorporated two existing lilacs flanking the front door of the main house and these were followed by *Mahonia aquifolium* under the windows and *Viburnum tinus* at either corner of the front of the house. China roses and rosemary were planted on one side of the building, leading to the small rose garden which was also designed to incorporate a herb border.

Jekyll was interested to learn what type of fencing would enclose the garden: 'What is the usual fencing from the road — nothing shows in the illustration. The usual thing for this class of house in England for the last 200 years is a fencing of upright slats about ½ inch thick pointed at the top either hard wood or oak for preference or white painted with posts at intervals of about 9 feet'. The reply from Miss Jennings was: 'The matter of putting up a suitable fence is being considered — but it has not been decided what kind it should be'. I have shown a white painted fence separating the hedge from the road with a small gate shown open at the angle it appears on Jekyll's plan.

The richly planted herbaceous borders which followed the outer boundaries of the plot complement the unpretentious elegance of the building. Jekyll has used many of her favourite plants. Lavender is planted on either side of the path at the entrance to the garden with *Stachys olympica* and bergenia. The colour scheme in the borders flanking the front gate entrance is soft and muted. White iris, dahlias and hollyhocks, *Lilium candidum, Chrysanthemum maximum*, the blooms of philadelphus and *Hebe brachysiphon* give a white emphasis to the scheme. The coolness of some white flowers is enhanced by the blue of campanulas, geraniums and lavenders and the creamy-toned white blooms have warmth added to them by the presence of pink snapdragons and hollyhocks, pinks, and dicentra.

At the far end of the border and round the next corner, *Fuchsia magellanica* 'Gracilis' with its red and violet pendulous flowers and grey-toned leaves bridges the gap between the muted colours and the brighter yellows and reds of the far border. Rudbeckia, helenium, oenothera, yellow iris and golden variegated euonymus give a sunlit glow to this border and combine with red hollyhocks and dahlias, richly dark snapdragons and bronze iris to give a sumptuous show of colour. Jekyll, once again, has based her design on the progression of tones and colours found in the colour spectrum. The backing for the red and gold border is common laurel, variegated golden holly and deep green Portugal laurel (*Prunus lusitanica*) and the house and garden are shown in my painting through a screen of Western red cedar (*Thuja plicata*) and Lawson cypress (*Chamaecyparis lawsoniana*).

Chapter Five

Plant Associations

ALTHOUGH COLOUR appeared to be the predominant feature of Jekyll's design with plants – and this was, perhaps, a natural bias for a garden designer originally trained as a painter – she also emphasised the importance of form and shape in planting. Here too she made an analogy with the world of art, comparing the arrangement of groups of plants to 'drawing', by which she meant the 'right movement of line and form and group'. This quality, she maintained, would be instantly recognisable to a sensitive gardener and particularly to one who was in sympathy with her own particular gardening philosophy. In contrast, an inadequately conceived arrangement of plants, lacking a sense of balance and proportion, with an absence of that quality of good 'drawing', would never create a pleasing composition.

Jekyll devoted a chapter to form in planting in *Colour in the Flower Garden*. But although she described in essence what she meant by a successful grouping of plants, she avoided the difficult task of explaining how to achieve that perfect blend of line, shape and proportion. These qualities, she admitted, were sometimes elusive even to acquaintances of hers who had been trained as artists. She criticised the instructions often given to contemporary gardeners about the grouping of plants in 'stiff blocks', but she herself failed in the chapter to provide her readers with anything beyond vague advice, relying on their empathy with her own gardening ideals.

Jekyll directed her readers to design each arrangement of plants with 'absolute conviction': one assumes that by this she meant grouping plants in the bold drifts which are a feature of her garden plans. She also emphasised the importance of blending groups of plants into their natural surroundings. Her own choice of plants for different areas of the garden and the way in which they were arranged reflected Jekyll's skill as a designer, not only with colour, but with plant form and texture. Here she demonstrated the bold conviction that she had tried, rather imprecisely, to convey to her readers, showing how her training readily enabled her to compose an arrangement of plants, their relative heights and shapes, into a pleasing and well-structured picture. Any artist soon learns that no amount of attractive detail will compensate for a poor composition; this, no doubt, is what Jekyll hoped her readers would understand. A bold use of plants assembled in generous groups, mixing different foliage forms and textures, placing dark foliage against light and architectural shapes against a soft mass of blooms, would create garden pictures which were full of life and interest. Sometimes groups of plants benefited from being composed within a formal structure but, by planting them in fluidly shaped drifts, the boring and predictable symmetry of the 'stiff blocks' which Jekyll decried could be avoided.

The illustrations in this chapter show groups of plants taken from the garden

XVIII. Seasonal plant groups ranging from early spring to autumn

A. *Helleborus orientalis*, epimedium and primroses.   **B.** *Vitis vinifera* 'Purpurea', the rose 'Blush Rambler'.   **C.** *Paeonia suffruticosa, Artemisia arborescens*.   **D.** *Cytisus scoparius, Lupinus arboreus, Euphorbia wulfenii*.   **E.** *Pyracantha coccinea* 'Lalandei', *Campsis radicans*.   **F.** *Viburnum opulus, Skimmia japonica*.

paintings in this book. As the groups are taken out of their garden context, I have been unable to show them planted in drifts but, instead, I have focused attention on the mixture of plant shapes and textures within each arrangement and on the relationship of one plant to another. The first series of individual paintings show seasonal arrangements of plants from early spring to autumn. The second set of paintings illustrates Jekyll's use of architectural plant forms which were designed to give structure and definition to each plant group.

The seasonal plant groups begin with an arrangement of spring plants. The Lenten rose, *Helleborus orientalis*, is planted together with the native primrose and epimedium to create a blend of subdued flower colours and an attractive mixture of foliage: the fresh green leaves of the primrose, the dark green foliage of the hellebores and the little heart shapes of the epimedium leaves delicately touched with pinkish red. An early summer combination of climbers, recommended for a pergola, shows Jekyll's favourite 'Claret Vine', *Vitis vinifera* 'Purpurea', mingled with the rose 'Blush Rambler' with its cascades of blush pink roses. The strongly-shaped leaves of the vine emphasise the fragile appearance of the tiny clustered rose blooms. A second early summer plant group features the showy bowl-shaped flowers of a tree peony, *Paeonia suffruticosa*, set off to advantage by the silver deeply-cut leaves of *Artemisia arborescens*.

An intricately textured group of plants continues the seasonal sequence through spring and early summer. Two plants with similar pea-like flowers, but contrasting shapes and habits, the broom *Cytisus scoparius* and the tree lupin *Lupinus arboreus*, are grouped together with *Euphorbia wulfenii*. The combination of plant form makes this a distinctive group, full of variety and interest, with a blend of yellows in the flowers and in the bracts of the euphorbia which unifies the plant arrangement.

Two early autumn plant arrangements end the series of seasonal paintings. In both of these combinations a bright crop of berries is the predominant feature. The firethorn, *Pyracantha coccinea* 'Lalandei', which Jekyll recommended for the wall of a cloistered arcade, is planted next to the trumpet vine, *Campsis radicans*. The orange-red of the clustered pyracantha berries is echoed again in the red trumpets of the vine. The two plants provide a contrast in habit: the stiff spiky formality of the pyracantha set against the sinuous twining of the vine. In the final group both plants show a profusion of berries. The guelder rose, *Viburnum opulus*, which Jekyll recommended for its fine crop of autumn fruit, is planted close to the evergreen *Skimmia japonica* and one presupposes that male and female varieties of skimmia were planted adjacently so that berries would be generously produced. The contrast here is provided by the free habit of the guelder rose, its leaves just on the turn, and the structured form of the skimmia with its shiny evergreen foliage.

Many of the plants which I have described in this first series of illustrations have architectural forms; but, in the second set of paintings, which appear on page 70, a strongly defined shape gives a markedly architectural character to most of the plants featured in the groups.

The combinations of these architectural plants start with an association of climbers which, apart from their distinctive leaf shapes, could also be recommended for their display of rich autumn colour. These two climbers, the boldly-leafed *Vitis coignetiae* twining with Virginia creeper (*Parthenocissus quinquefolia*), were recommended by Jekyll for pergolas although both plants produce such rampant growth that they could only be suitable for the large solid structures, supported on stone or brick piers, which became such a feature of Edwardian gardens. The second group of plants combines a shrub and two rock plants. *Olearia phlogopappa* with its upright panicles of daisy-like flowers forms a background for the glaucous sculptured leaves of *Othonna cheirifolia* (syn. *Othonnopsis cheirifolia*) which stand out against the massed white flowers of the olearia. *Sedum spurium* forms a mat of bright green leaf-rosettes in front of the othonnopsis.

An attractive combination of plants for waterside planting is the ostrich feather fern, *Matteuccia struthiopteris*, and purple blue *Iris sibirica*. Their foliage would add definition to the margins of a pool: the unfurled fronds of the fern contrasting with the spiky leaves of the iris. Broader strappy spikes of foliage surround the cream plumes of Jekyll's favourite architectural plant, the yucca. In this case *Yucca gloriosa* is planted with rosemary and China roses. The rosemary's less obvious architectural habit nevertheless contrasts with the tumbling mass of soft pink rose blooms in an association of plants which was frequently used by Jekyll.

Acanthus spinosus combines with *Eryngium* x *oliverianum* to create an association of plants with a distinctively sculptural character. The deeply-cut shiny leaves and bold flower spikes of the acanthus and the blue teasel-like heads of the eryngium surrounded by their spiny bracts are combined with the massed heads of dwarf lavender to provide an association of plants which individually all have a sharply defined habit.

The final group of plants was designed for a semi-wild garden. The tall curving stems of Solomon's seal, *Polygonatum* x *hybridum*, bend over a generous clump of bergenia. Jekyll used both *Bergenia cordifolia* and *Bergenia ligulata* mainly as foliage plants. She even recommended removing the blooms of *Bergenia cordifolia* so that all the strength of the plant would remain in the leaves. *Iris foetidissima* completes the group. Its evergreen leaves and delicate flowers have a subtle appeal which is particularly suitable for a wild garden but Jekyll would also have planted this native iris for its autumn display of decorative seed pods bursting with bright berries.

The common feature of all the plant groups I have painted is the diversity of interest which Jekyll achieved by grouping these plants together. The textures of leaves, the shapes of flowers, the differences in plant height and habit all combined to create, in the context of their garden setting, the garden pictures which Jekyll sought to compose.

XIX. Architectural plant groups

G. *Vitis coignetiae, Parthenocissus quinquefolia*. **H**. *Olearia phlogopappa, Othonna cheirifolia* (syn. *Othonnopsis cheirifolia*), *Sedum spurium*. **I**. *Matteuccia struthiopteris, Iris sibirica*. **J**. *Yucca gloriosa*, China roses, rosemary. **K**. *Acanthus spinosus, Eryngium × oliverianum*, dwarf lavender. **L**. *Polygonatum × hybridum, Bergenia cordifolia, Iris foetidissima*.

Chapter Six

Ornament and Architectural Detail

THE TWO GARDENS illustrated in this chapter are similar in that they were both designed for steeply sloping sites which involved some dramatic hard landscaping. The nature of the sites demanded a structured and architectural approach to the design with terraced retaining walls, steps and paths being constructed as essential preliminary features before the gardens could begin to be planted. The first garden, in Surrey, still exists today with most of its design intact. The second garden, planned for two wealthy Americans in Ohio, has an intriguing story attached to it and, in fact, was never implemented.

Fox Hill is an attractive white-painted Edwardian family house at Elstead in Surrey, not far from Jekyll's own home. Only four plans remain of the original designs for this unusual terraced garden of about two to three acres produced by Jekyll for her client, Mrs. Hamilton, in 1923. However, these cover most of the planting and clearly illustrate the hard landscaping of the site. Fortunately, most of the terraced retaining walls, built of local Bargate stone, and the steps and paths in the garden are still in excellent condition as they have been carefully maintained over the years.

The most important feature of the terrace structures is a curved wall with steps leading up on either side to the higher levels of the garden. In the centre of this facade and set into the wall is the handsome lion mask shown in Jekyll's drawing. Its gaping mouth cunningly hides a water spout which spills water into a small almond-shaped pool below. This delightful feature is still in perfect working order. The lion mask is almost identical to the one illustrated in *Gardens for Small Country Houses* for a tile-built fountain designed by Lutyens. That mask was modelled by a talented sculptress of the day – a good friend and neighbour of Jekyll's, Lady Julia Chance, the owner of Orchards, Godalming – so it is likely that the Fox Hill mask was produced by the same hand.

The original plans show a rather curious siting for a sundial, which was placed projecting into the centre of the little pool. In this position, it would have detracted from the lion mask and dominated the pool. The owners of Fox Hill, when I visited the garden, obviously felt this to be the case because they had resited the sundial elsewhere in the garden. But I have, for the sake of accuracy, illustrated it in its original position.

There is no existing evidence of an architect's involvement with this site, so it is possible that Jekyll may have designed the whole garden including the hard landscaping. The steeply sloping site must have presented Jekyll with a challenge. This is not a big garden and very little of it is at ground level. The flat part of the garden is laid out to lawn but there was, at one time, a long herbaceous border running along the length of the main grassed area. The first level is reached by the two flights of steps behind the curved wall with the water spout. These steps join into a single flight which leads upwards to a vantage point with stone seating. The area on either side of this feature is quite generous and allowed Jekyll the scope she needed to create an exciting display of planting. Paths, punctuated by flights of steps, continue upwards encircling the vantage point and eventually become part of an informal network of tracks leading through the woodland which overlooks the garden. Soil has now covered some of these paths and so excavation would be required to expose them to view again.

Jekyll's choice of plants suggests that the soil was well drained and that the conditions were similar to heathland. Acid-loving plants like rhododendrons and tree heaths obviously suited the site and there are still some of Jekyll's original rhododendrons in the garden today. The first terrace above ground level was richly planted with a variety of shrubs: Jekyll's favourite Scotch briar roses, native wild plants and a mass of lavender, santolina and nepeta on top of the wall. The wall itself was planted with rock plants rooted in crevices among the stones. These plants would have formed generous clumps tumbling down over the face of the wall. I have shown the garden in early summer when the finest display of plants could have been seen and my viewpoint is above normal eye level in order to convey an impression of the mass of planting.

Jekyll planned a colour scheme that was limited to a variety of blues, whites, pink and yellow flowers with greys, glaucous tints and soft textures in the foliage. The plants are massed in large numbers to create an impressive effect. There is a generous planting of *Cistus laurifolius* and *Cistus* x *cyprius*, tamarisk, sea buckthorn (*Hippophae rhamnoides*) and *Rhododendron ponticum*. This rhododendron still exists in the garden. A large area is planted out with tree lupins (*Lupinus arboreus*). I have shown these in the yellow shade favoured by Jekyll herself in *Colour in the Flower Garden* – 'Its best colour is a clear, lively light yellow' – and in front of these plants is an important display of *Euphorbia wulfenii* and *Cassinia fulvida* with its gold-tinted tiny evergreen leaves. Fourteen Scotch briars (*Rosa pimpinellifolia*) are planted behind groups of *Senecio greyi*, *Olearia phlogopappa* and dwarf lavenders. Jekyll also includes large quantities of 'yellow broom' but she does not specify whether this should be a variety of cytisus or genista or whether she has in mind *Spartium junceum*, 'the yellow Spanish broom', which she recommended in *Wall, Water and Woodland Gardens* as an indispensible variety. Yellow is a predominant colour of the scheme and is repeated again in a group of *Kerria japonica*, not in flower at this time, and in the tall candelabra of verbascum.

Behind the enclosed area of the vantage point is planted *Hebe brachysiphon* and above this is a group of tree heaths, *Erica australis* and *Erica lusitanica*. I have not been able to show the full shrub planting above this point because of the limits of my view, but I have sketched in the woodland which exists today and would have provided the background to Jekyll's planting. When I first saw this garden, I imagined the overall effect that her planting scheme would have created and I have tried to capture it in my painting. Against the darker woodland, the pale colours of the flowers and predominance of yellow blooms stand out and give a permanent impression of brightness and sunlight.

The second garden I have painted, Elmhurst, was the first of three American gardens designed by Jekyll. She began to produce designs for her clients, Mr. and Mrs. Glendinning B. Groesbeck in 1914. Grace Groesbeck was a devotee of Jekyll's work, like many contemporary Americans interested in the design of gardens. In a letter to Jekyll, Grace Groesbeck wrote: 'I have reread your latest work and feel that I am very fortunate in having secured your consent to plan our place'. Jekyll's work through her writing was already well-known in America and a number of American authors interpreted Jekyll's planting and gardening philosophy for their own readers, adapting her ideas to local gardening conditions. Jekyll never travelled to America but she had a large number of visitors from the USA at Munstead Wood and it is evident that, during the course of her working life, she formed many friendships with Americans who shared her passion for gardens and garden plants.

The Groesbecks both came from prominent Cincinnati families. Glendinning Groesbeck owed his inheritance to his grandfather, William Groesbeck, a successful lawyer of his day and a well known orator. Grace [Seely] Groesbeck was the daughter of a wealthy and highly respected Cincinnati doctor and she was able to bring her own considerable personal fortune to the marriage at a time when her husband's finances were in decline. The Groesbeck family house, a large Victorian mansion named Elmhurst, had become dilapidated through lack of funds and so, with this timely injection of Seely money, the newly married couple decided to acquire a large plot of land at Perintown on which to build a new house set among woodland with views over the Ohio countryside. As Grace Groesbeck wrote in a letter to Jekyll: 'A good view can be obtained from any part of the ground shown'.

Several sets of plans were produced; twenty-seven individual drawings make up the sets. I have counted four different schemes and each set of plans showed adventurous and complex designs involving elaborate terracing with water-lily pools and tanks, steps leading to shrub lined walks in between levels, formal lawns and rock gardens. The hard landscaping in itself was a major undertaking.

While planning their new home, the Groesbecks lived in an apartment in Elmhurst, the original Groesbeck mansion, and perhaps they intended to maintain this continuity by naming their new house Elmhurst as it appears on Jekyll's plans. However, although the Groesbecks did eventually build their new house, it could not be built on the site shown on Jekyll's plans. It seems incredible that the Groesbecks did not begin by having a very thorough survey made of their chosen site before commissioning Jekyll to produce so many different planting schemes for their proposed garden. As it later proved, the site was too unstable to support the new house, let alone the complex series of terraces descending down the side of this steep valley.

The house was eventually built about a hundred yards away on a flat site, and by this stage, Grace Groesbeck decided to plan her own garden. She designed a garden which was influenced by both Jekyll and Beatrix Farrand and as she was one of the founder members of the Cincinnati Gardening Club, her garden was regarded as one of the finest in the county. Nothing much remains of her original garden today. Like so many of Jekyll's own gardens, the original planting has gone and only the bare bones of the garden remain: the granite pillared round garden, originally a rose garden, with its paths leading away in four directions, granite edging which once marked out flower

XX. Fox Hill Terraced Garden

A steeply terraced garden in Surrey with an intricate arrangement of hard landscaping in stone. A small pool with a lion's-head water spout provides the central focus of the garden. Steps lead up behind the curved wall with the water spout to a vantage point. The areas on either side

of the steps are planted with a wide variety of shrubs. Lavender fringes the steps and, together with senecio and nepeta, overhangs the walls. Rock plants cover the surface of the wall on the right of the painting. The colour scheme of pale colours, with a predominance of yellow, stands out against the background of dark woodland above the garden.

Fox Hill Terraced Garden (pages 74–5)

1. *Senecio greyi (Brachyglottis greyi).*
2. Lavender = *Lavandula angustifolia*
3. Nepeta = *Nepeta × faassenii.*
4. Cistus = *Cistus laurifolius.*
5. Verbascum = *Verbascum olympicum.*
6. Saponaria = *Saponaria officinalis.*
7. Yellow broom = *Cytisus scoparius.*
8. *Veronica traversii (Hebe brachysiphon).*
9. Scotch briars *(Rosa pimpinellifolia).*
10. *Olearia gunniana (O. phlogopappa).*
11. *Othonna cheirifolia (syn. Othonnopsis cheirifolia).*
12. *Sedum spurium.*
13. Rock pinks.
14. Cerastium.
15. *Iris stylosa (syn I. unguicularis).*
16. *Plumbago larpentae (Ceratostigma plumbaginoides).*
17. Helianthemum.
18. *Scabiosa pterocephala (Pterocephala perennis perennis).*
19. Iberis = *Iberis sempervirens.*
20. *Epimedium pinnatum.*
21. Dwarf lavender = *Lavandula angustifolia* 'Hidcote' (syn. *L. nana atropurpurea).*
22. Santolina = *Santolina chamaecyparissus.*
23. Cassinia = *Cassinia fulvida.*
24. Tamarisk = *Tamarix gallica.*
25. *Cistus × cyprius.*
26. Hippophae = *Hippophae rhamnoides.*

27. Tree lupin = *Lupinus arboreus.*
28. *Euphorbia wulfenii.*
29. *Kerria japonica.*
30. *Cistus laurifolius.*
31. *Erica lusitanica.*
32. *Erica australis.*
33. *Alisma plantago-aquatica.*

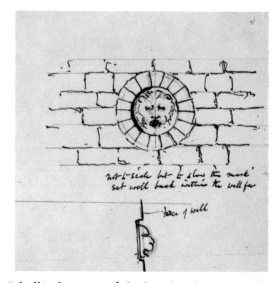

Jekyll's drawing of the lion-head at Fox Hill

borders, and steps to a sunken garden. After her death, Grace Groesbeck willed her estate to the Girl Scouts of America. Ten years later it was sold to the Presbyterian Church and today it is the Wildwood Christian Education Center. The rose garden site is now used for Christian counselling, services and meetings.

It must have been a disappointment for Jekyll that her plans were never implemented. This was her first American commission and, if realized as planned, would have been a spectacular garden and a wonderful example of her work. She had started a notebook for Elmhurst but this remained empty of plant lists. The entries only included descriptions of the proposed interior of the new house, and the comment that there was plenty of stone available for dry stone walling from the creek at the lowest level of the site and 'plenty of virgin loam from the woods'. Grace Groesbeck refers to the loam herself 'which can be used where needed' as a supplement to the thin sandy soil of the area.

I have shown in my painting how Jekyll's fourth scheme might have appeared from a high perspective viewpoint. In the distance one can see a hint of the woodland surrounding the original site with the woodland walks that Grace Groesbeck was particularly keen to have as part of the design. I have shown the garden in summer. Stone is indicated for the hard landscaping and, if the garden had been implemented, this would probably have been a local stone, perhaps the same granite which was used for the hard landscaping in Grace Groesbeck's garden.

Only three levels of the plan are shown so that the water lily pool is not at ground level. The pool was shaped to repeat the curved design of the flights of steps which led down from a projecting balcony above. From here, one could overlook the water and admire Jekyll's choice of water lilies which included: *Nymphaea* 'Marliacea Carnea', *Nymphaea* 'Marliacea Rosea' and *Nymphaea* 'Marliacea Chromatella'. I have shown the surrounding area of the pool with gaps among the paving stones to provide planting spaces for wall shrubs and climbers. There is a grape vine on one wall. Jekyll was particularly fond of a 'red-leaved Claret vine' which was probably *Vitis vinifera* 'Purpurea', so I have made this my choice. Its leaves would have picked up the reddish tone of the leaves of *Nymphaea* 'Marliacea Carnea'. Next to the vine is jasmine, then *Robinia hispida* and on either side of the balcony projection, there are plantings of bay. *Ceanothus* 'Gloire de Versailles' can just be seen in the picture.

The next terrace up shows a gravel walk, leading to a lawn edged with *Skimmia japonica*. Borders flank the gravelled area, with on one side a border of rosemary, lavender and China roses (I have shown 'Old Blush', the old pink China rose that Jekyll favoured). *Yucca recurvifolia* grow among the China roses and the wichuriana hybrid rose 'Jersey Beauty' is planted to fall over the wall on the far side giving something of interest to enjoy while walking up the flight of steps from the water lily pool. Beyond 'Jersey Beauty' are planted *Rosa virginiana* and its double hybrid form 'Rose d'Amour'.

Opposite this border and in the centre of the terrace wall is a *Magnolia grandiflora* with vines (again, I have shown *Vitis vinifera* 'Purpurea') and *Olearia phlogopappa* planted on either side of it, followed by lavender and *Choisya ternata*. The border is enclosed by stone-built boxes on either side of the ascending flights of steps. Jekyll does not indicate how these were to be planted but I have shown them planted with yuccas. In her plan for the terraced garden of Walsham House in Surrey (see Chapter Eight), Jekyll shows

XXI. Elmhurst Architectural Terraced Garden

Jekyll's first American commission in 1914, a garden of architectural character in Ohio, was never implemented due to the instability of its steeply sloping site. The painting shows three levels of the garden. The water lily pool in the left-hand corner of the picture is overlooked by

a balcony. On the next level, borders of shrubs including roses, lavender, rosemary and a *Magnolia grandiflora* are separated by a gravel walk leading to a lawn edged with skimmias. Stone containers filled with yuccas stand on either side of ascending flights of steps. At the highest level in the painting there is a rockery and ornamental pool. A pathway leads away into distant woodland.

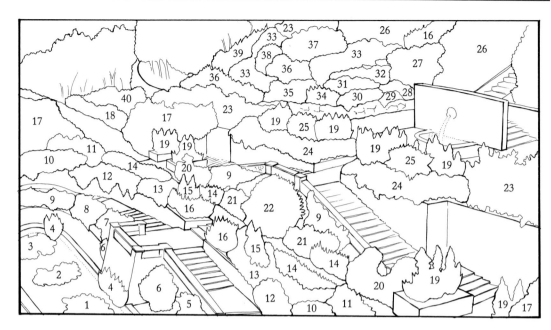

Elmhurst Terraced Architectural
Garden (pages 78–9)

1. *Nymphaea* 'Marliacea Rosea'.
2. *Nymphaea* 'Marliacea Chromatella'.
3. *Nymphaea* 'Marliacea Carnea'.
4. Water plantain = *Alisma plantago-aquatica*.
5. *Ceanothus* 'Gloire de Versailles'.
6. Bay = *Laurus nobilis*.
7. *Robinia hispida*.
8. White jasmine = *Jasminum officinalis*.
9. Grape vine trained on wall = *Vitis vinifera* 'Purpurea'.
10. *Rosa lucida* type (*R. virginiana*).
11. 'Rose d'Amour' = *Rosa virginiana plena*.
12. Rose 'Jersey Beauty'.
13. China roses = 'Old Blush'.
14. Lavender = *Lavandula angustifolia*.
15. *Yucca recurvifolia*.
16. Rosemary.
17. Box = *Buxus*.
18. *Skimmia oblata* (*S. japonica*. [* Grow *S. veitchii*, male, with *S.* 'Highgrove Red Bud', female, for berries: ◊ *S. japonica* 'Formanii', flowers usually female, but some bisexual flowers occur.])
19. *Yucca filamentosa* [Yuccas in boxes are my choice. See Chapter Eight, Walsham House, Pages 94/95].
20. *Choisya ternata*.
21. *Olearia gunniana* (*O. phlogopappa*).
22. *Magnolia grandiflora*.
23. *Berberis aquifolium* (*Mahonia aquifolium*).
24. Scotch briars (*Rosa pimpinellifolia*).
25. *Yucca gloriosa*.

26. Laurustinus (*Viburnum tinus*).
27. *Cistus laurifolius*.
28. Iberis = *Iberis sempervirens*.
29. *Phlox subulata*.
30. Lithospermum = *Lithospermum diffusum* (syn. *Lithodora diffusa*).
31. *Othonna cheirifolia* (syn. *Othonnopsis cheirifolia*).
32. Cotoneaster = *Cotoneaster horizontalis*.
33. Rambling roses = 'The Garland', 'Dundee Rambler'. See *Roses for English Gardens*, Chapter XI, 'Roses As Fountains And Growing Free'.
34. *Veronica prostrata*.
35. *Plumbago larpentae* (*Ceratostigma plumbaginoides*).
36. *Pernettya mucronata*.
37. *Rhus cotinus* (*Cotinus coggygria*).
38. Berberis [illegible].
39. *Tamarisk gallica* = *Tamarix gallica*.
40. *Rosa multiflora* – single blooms.

an identical design of container for yuccas. This choice of planting would have provided continuity and a visual balance in her design for the Elmhurst terraces, as yuccas already feature prominently in the opposite border and on the upper terrace.

The upper level in the painting shows another gravel walk eventually leading into a woodland path. Borders of *Yucca filamentosa* and *Yucca gloriosa* surrounded by Scotch briars extend into a hedge-like planting of *Mahonia aquifolium*, then fresh green box and *Rosa multiflora*, creating a semi-wild transition between formal garden and woodland. A striking feature is a small six-sided tank backed by a wall. I have used some artistic licence here as this design is so similar to the fountain pool in the previous garden, Fox Hill, that I have painted a fountain head in the centre of the wall. I do not believe it would have been left unadorned, even if the sculpture was not used as a water spout. Stairs lead up behind the wall to the terrace on the same level as the house.

The other dominant feature is a rock garden. Rock plants fall over the rocks and there is a predominance of blue flowers, perhaps to give a sense of coolness on a hot summer's day: lithodora (syn. lithospermum), *Veronica prostrata, Ceratostigma plumbaginoides* and the glaucous leaves of *Othonna cheirifolia* (syn. *Othonnopsis cheirifolia*). *Phlox subulata* and double arabis are also to be planted here. Beyond, cotoneaster (I have shown *Cotoneaster horizontalis*) spreads itself over the ground and behind it Jekyll suggests rambling roses; where these are marked on the plan, I have shown her favourite, 'The Garland': 'Among the many ways of worthily using the free Ayrshire Roses, one of the best is to leave them their own way of growth, without any staking or guiding whatever... Of these useful garden Roses none is more beautiful than the Garland, with its masses of pretty blush-white bloom' (*Roses For English Gardens*).

White-flowered *Cistus laurifolius* is also planted here along with evergreen *Viburnum tinus*, pernettya, rosemary and *Mahonia aquifolium*. *Cotinus coggygria* is shown in flower and so is a swathe of tamarisk which separates the formal garden from woodland.

It will be apparent to anyone who is familiar with the climate of the region that much of Jekyll's planting would not have survived an Ohio winter. She admitted her own ignorance of weather conditions and climate in America; so in this respect too, the gardens at Elmhurst would have been impractical to implement. Jekyll would have had to revise much of her planting plan, probably under the guidance of local horticultural experts and nurserymen.

Chapter Seven

Garden Designs with Water

J EKYLL'S ENTHUSIASM for water features in the garden is evident in her writings. Whether she is describing the planting of natural pool or lake margins, the banks of a stream or an arrangement of water lilies in a formal pool or tank, her delight and 'pleasure in true water-gardening' is apparent. The contemporary passion for water lilies led Jekyll to comment that even the 'homeliest' garden now had its water lily tank, so in this chapter I have featured two examples which I feel have particular charm.

The circular water lily tank garden with its surround of yew hedging still remains one of the most distinctive features of the gardens at Watlington Park (see Chapter One). But the tank has now been cleared of its once profuse planting of water lilies and, although it is too shallow for swimming, it is used as a place to cool off on a hot summer's day. This seems to have always been an Esher family tradition, because an old photograph exists in the family's album of Viscount Esher, the present owner's grandfather, armpit-deep in a mass of water lilies.

But the Eshers must have felt that the surroundings of the pool could be improved for it was proposed that Jekyll should redesign this area. She was sent a photograph of the tank garden by Antoinette Brett who described it as 'a rather bad photograph of the lily pond, which has a paved path planted with rock plants, a brick wall ditto & behind that a grass path with on one side a big yew hedge & on the others a Dorothy Perkins – all these running round the pond in a circle'. With the exception of the roses, which were removed and replaced by a continuation of the yew hedging, it is interesting to see that the present tank garden appears very much as it did in this contemporary photograph. There is no certain indication from the layout of the garden today that the scheme whch Jekyll designed was ever implemented.

Jekyll's plan for the garden was to introduce borders round the top of the wall surrounding the pool. The rock plants which Antoinette Brett mentions in her letter were obviously to be left in place and so are not identified in Jekyll's drawings for the garden. For this reason I have had to leave them out of my painting. As there was no suggestion of the varieties of water lily planted in the pool, I have restricted my choice in my painting to the common creamy yellow water lily.

Jekyll chose a rich variety of chalk-tolerant plants for the borders surrounding the pool. These were designed to give interest throughout the seasons, starting in the spring with *Omphalodes verna, Anemone sylvestris* and bergenia. Two clumps of *Helleborus orientalis* were to be planted on either side of one flight of steps leading down to the paved area round the pool; drifts of viola, possibly Jekyll's favourite early-flowering sweet violet, *Viola odorata*, were planted on top of the wall. These spring plants were followed by epimedium, dicentra, aquilegia and iris.

XXII. Widford Octagonal Water Lily Pool Garden

Widford Octagonal Water Lily Pool
Garden (page 83)

1. *Rhododendron ferrugineum.*
2. *Kalmia latifolia.*
3. Irish yew = *Taxus baccata* 'Fastigiata'.
4. *Andromeda axillaris (Leucothoë axillaris).*
5. *Andromeda catesbaei (Leucothoë fontanesiana).*
6. *Spiraea lindleyana (Sorbaria Lindleyana* [syn. *S. tomentosa*]).
7. Aesculus = horse chestnut.
8. Laurustinus *(Viburnum tinus).*
9. *Alisma plantago-aquatica.*
10. Water lilies.

My painting shows the garden in June when I feel the borders would have appeared at their best. I have taken a view looking down on the pool so that the layout and shape of the garden can be clearly seen. A predominantly grey or blue-grey foliage colour scheme is provided by lavenders, *Artemisia ludoviciana* and hostas. I have chosen to illustrate *Hosta sieboldiana* as the blue-green leaves fit in with the colour scheme provided by the rest of the planting. Unfortunately Jekyll does not specify the species she would have chosen for this plan. The soft grey-toned leaves of *Senecio greyi* and *Phlomis fruticosa* also form part of this scheme, with the leaves of *Eryngium giganteum* adding to the shades of blue foliage. At the deeper end of this colour spectrum there are the dark leaves of purple sage. Shrubs include familiar Jekyll favourites: there are generous groups of *Hebe brachysiphon*, Scotch briars (*Rosa pimpinellifolia*) and the rose, 'Blush Damask'.

The grey and blue shades of foliage are echoed in the cool colours of the flowers. There is the misty lavender blue of nepeta, the stronger tones of *Veronica prostrata* and *Geranium grandiflorum*, (now known as *G. himalayense*) and the purple-blue of *Iris sibirica*. Setting off the blues to advantage are the warm yellows of senecio and phlomis, the creamy blooms of the Scotch briars and a variety of pastel pinks. The pink spectrum starts with the delicate shades of the rock pinks and deepens into the soft pink of the blooms of 'Blush Damask'. Then there are the stronger tones of the dicentra (I have shown *Dicentra eximia*), aquilegia and valerian. The final touch to this subtle colour scheme is added by the white flowers of arabis, *Campanula persicifolia*, *Hebe brachysiphon*, white tree lupin and the blooms of gypsophila which would have veiled nearby plants in a dense mist of tiny dots. Jekyll also chose a number of fragrant plants as the effect of scent would have been intensified by the enclosure of the garden.

The pool garden at Widford, in Surrey, was designed by Jekyll for her client Henry Barrett in 1925. It was planned to be sited in a field that Barrett had acquired as an extension to his garden. Seven plans for this site still remain. The main garden which already existed in the nineteen twenties had been laid out, it is thought, by a firm of local surveyors. Unfortunately, the whole site is now divided into three plots and this has disrupted the cohesion of the original design. Nevertheless the pool garden remains a distinctive example of Jekyll's work.

Jekyll's commission was to design a scheme for the field and link it to the established layout of the existing garden. In a letter from his London address in Albemarle Street, Barrett wrote: 'What I want is some idea of what to do with the whole centre of the field... I do not want any more flower beds, as I think it would give too much work for the gardeners, and I have plenty in the existing garden, which is nearer to the house. I should not object to some Rock-work, or a Fountain, or beds of trees or shrubs, as they would not entail very much additional work'.

The correspondence between Barrett and Jekyll was business-like. He gave the impression of being a man who was impatient with any delay once he had made up his mind to proceed with a project. There is only one letter from Jekyll about the pool garden and one must assume that any other letters may have been lost:

You will already have got a considerable variety of trees and shrubs in what you have already planted & I thought that in this garden it might be well to keep to something restful. I therefore advise in the outer spaces a considerable planting of Rhododendrons of a few beautiful kinds in the upper [illegible] & of Azaleas in the lower. The angles being filled with trees as shown... Of the 4 clumps bordering the tank I have only filled in one as they shall all be treated alike.

I have chosen to illustrate the central core of the pool garden with a view of the octagonal pool, still in good condition except for slight leakage, and part of the two shrubberies beyond. The pool was at the heart of the design and was surrounded by four shrubberies of identical shape. These planting areas were quartered by paths which led through into the garden beyond. It was an unusual idea to have a formal feature like a pool in such a position, remote from the main part of the garden and in the centre of informal shrub planting. It gives the site a mysterious atmosphere like that of a secret garden.

The shape of the shrub borders is rather formally structured, but the richness of the planting would have disguised the shapes of the beds. The soil is acid in this garden and

XXIII. Watlington Park Water Lily Tank Garden

The painting shows a bird's eye view of the circular garden, enclosed by thick yew hedging, with its generous-sized water lily tank. Jekyll's plan for the redesign in 1922 of this Oxfordshire garden introduced borders round the top of the wall surrounding the pool. The

rose 'Blush Damask' flanks the steps in the foreground of the painting and also the flight directly opposite across the pool. Jekyll chose a delicate colour scheme of pink, blue, pale yellow and white. She mixed together roses, hebes and lavender and grey-leaved plants such as phlomis and senecio with clouds of white gypsophila, misty blue nepeta and chalk-loving plants like valerian and pinks.

Watlington Park Water Lily Tank
Garden (pages 86–7)

1. Rose 'Blush Gallica' ('Blush Damask').
2. *Veronica traversii (Hebe brachysiphon).*
3. Scotch briars *(Rosa pimpinellifolia).*
4. Epimedium = *Epimedium pinnatum.*
5. Dicentra = *Dicentra eximia.*
6. *Geranium ibericum.*
7. Solomon's Seal = *Polygonatum* × *hybridum.*
8. Aquilegia.
9. Lenten hellebores = *Helleborus orientalis.*
10. *Anemone japonica.*
11. *Campanula carpatica.*
12. *Megasea ligulata (Bergenia ligulata* or * *B. schmidtii).*
13. *Iris sibirica.*
14. Viola = *Viola odorata.*
15. White *Campanula persicifolia = C. persicifolia alba.*
16. Funkia (hosta) = *Hosta sieboldiana.*
17. *Campanula macrantha (C. latifolia).*
18. *Geranium grandiflorum (G. himalayense).*
19. *Artemisia ludoviciana.*
20. Lavender = *Lavandula angustifolia.*
21. *Veronica rupestris (V. prostrata).*
22. Nepeta = *Nepeta* × *faassenii.*
23. Dwarf lavender = *Lavandula angustifolia* 'Hidcote' (syn. *L. nana atropurpurea).*
24. Gypsophila = *Gypsophila paniculata.*
25. White tree lupin = *Lupinus arboreus.*

26. Echinops = *Echinops ritro.*
27. *Eryngium giganteum.*
28. Euphorbia = *Euphorbia wulfenii.*
29. Erigeron.
30. *Sedum spurium.*
31. Pink pinks.
32. Purple sage = *Salvia officinalis* 'Purpurascens'.
33. *Phlomis fruticosa.*
34. *Senecio greyi (Brachyglottis greyi).*
35. Centranthus = *Centranthus ruber.*
36. Iris = tall bearded iris – 'Mrs. H. Darwin', white with inconspicuous violet veins [* no alternative colour match. Try 'Bridesmaid', white: ◊ 'Lacy Snowflake', 'Laced Cotton', 'Pontiff', 'Leda's Lover', 'Skier's Delight', all white].
37. Campanula [illegible].
38. *Phlox stellaria* [* *P.* 'G. F. Wilson'].
39. Double arabis.
40. Water lilies.

Jekyll chose a selection of acid-loving subjects.

The painting shows the garden in June. This is essentially a green garden with occasional colour provided by the seasonal flowering of shrubs. Here it is the pink blooms of late-flowering *Rhododendron ferrugineum* and the showy flowers of *Kalmia latifolia* which provide interest against the background of varied greens. Jekyll edged the shrub borders with *Leucothoë axillaris*. There is no record of the water lilies she may have suggested for the pool and I have illustrated the common water lilies present in the pool today. The design of the pool with its stone coping and central fountain was carefully specified by Jekyll to include adequate crevices among the stones of the fountain's supporting structure. These were to provide hiding places for the fish which were to stock the pool. Barrett was a keen collector of classical statuary and replaced Jekyll's simple basin and fountain, which I have illustrated, with a showy bronze Roman eagle.

Just inside the margins of the pool, on two sides of the octagon, there were to be enclosed areas filled with mud intended for aquatic plants. Jekyll does not specify these but her sketch indicates a hint of her favourite *Alisma plantago-aquatica*, so I have shown a simple edging of this plant.

The final garden in this chapter is a curiosity: it is a Japanese water garden which formed part of Jekyll's scheme for a garden in Worcestershire. Jekyll's client, Arthur Kenrick, twice engaged her to design schemes for his gardens. In this first instance her commission came through the architects Forbes & Tait whom he engaged in 1914 to redesign the grounds of his new home, Field House, Clent, near Stourbridge; nineteen plans for this still exist. From Field House, Kenrick moved in 1920 to Walsham House in Surrey (see Chapter Eight) where he kept Jekyll busy producing designs for the gardens over a period of nine years.

Following Kenrick's occupation of Field House for six years, the house and grounds were acquired in the nineteen-twenties by Ernest Vaughan, an industrialist. The house was then bought by Birmingham City Council and, at this stage, the gardens became locally well-known for their topiary, the creation of Harry Sherriff, the head gardener for thirty-five years. Today Field House has been turned into a rest home for the elderly. Of Kenrick nothing is known, but a brief note to Jekyll indicates that, like Henry Barrett, he was an impatient man: 'I have any quantity of Nepeta London Pride & white Pinks. I should want good strong stuff as I want to get an effect as soon as possible'.

The gardens have been well maintained but it is obvious that much of the original design has been lost or was never implemented. The plans include a sunken garden which exists today, although without the original planting. A delightful feature of this garden is the small orangery that still remains in good condition. Nothing appears to remain of the other schemes for the gardens – the tank garden, terraced borders, rose garden or, the most unusual design of all and the one which I have chosen for my painting, the Japanese water garden.

The architects' structural design for the water garden showed attention to details of drainage, and included a meticulous drawing showing a cross section of the sloping sectioned-off borders surrounding the pool and a detailed illustration of a Japanese bridge. Paving is indicated for the edging of the pool and I have copied the type of stone which was used in the sunken garden. I have shown the bridge made of wood, stained red in the manner of many oriental water garden bridges. The siting of this garden indicates that the little bridge spanned either a stream or a ha-ha. By crossing it one reached a semi-circular paved platform projecting into the half-moon or fan-shaped pool that is this garden's most distinctive architectural feature.

Jekyll's planting scheme for the borders is obviously intended to soften the structure of the garden, perhaps because she found its design too severe and architectural. Groups of *Aruncus dioicus* and *Filipendula rubra* disguise the hard outlines of the borders and their separating structures. Iris leaves provide a sharper emphasis, but the varieties she selected all have refined foliage: *Iris sibirica, I. orientalis* (syn *I. ochroleuca*) and *I. laevigata*. She introduced clumps of *Glyceria aquatica* and ferns to give foliage interest and the raised wall enclosing the borders is covered with rock plants.

The choice of plants indicates that the soil in this garden must have been moisture retentive and she records in her notebook that it was 'very rich soil'. So instead of rock garden plants which thrive in dry positions, Jekyll selected *Saxifraga* x *urbium* (London Pride), asarum and epimedium, vinca, myosotis and mimulus, all planted to spill over the low walls enclosing the garden. Perennial geraniums also feature in the planting plan and there are generous groupings of *Primula sikkimensis* which 'is a wonderful picture of plant beauty; the full heads of hanging sulphur bells having that curiously luminous quality that is only observed in this and one or two other flowers of this rare colouring' (*A Gardener's Testament*).

I have illustrated only a cross section of the garden but even with this limited view, shown in early June, the freshness and deceptive simplicity of the colour scheme is apparent. The predominant colours are yellow and blue with a variety of different greens in the foliage. The clear yellows give an oriental feel to the garden and they are perfectly enhanced by the blues, shown in an elegant choice of iris species and among the perennial geraniums.

The semi-circle of sloping borders is divided from the half-moon of water by a wide paved path. Round the edge of the pool there is inserted a planting area, separate from the pool itself, which was designed to be filled with aquatic plants. Jekyll chose the 'eminent beauty of the native water-side plants', the water plantain (*Alisma plantago-aquatica*), branched bur-reed (*Sparganium ramosum*), flowering rush (*Butomus umbellatus*), and the arrowhead (*Sagittaria sagittifolia*) rather than a display of water lilies. Perhaps she intended the pool to remain uncluttered, simply acting as a mirror to the sky, a peaceful place for quiet meditation, thereby creating the authentic atmosphere for a Japanese garden.

XXIV. Field House Japanese Water Garden

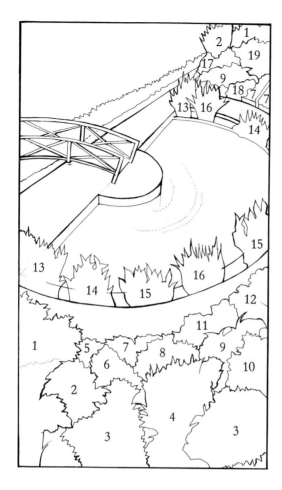

Field House Japanese Water Garden (page 91)

1. *Spiraea aruncus (Aruncus dioicus).*
2. *Iris sibirica.*
3. *Spiraea venusta (Filipendula rubra).*
4. *Iris laevigata.*
5. Asarum = *Asarum europaeum.*
6. Epimedium = *Epimedium pinnatum.*
7. Mimulus [illegible].
8. *Geranium ibericum.*
9. *Glyceria aquatica (G. maxima* 'Variegata').
10. *Iris orientalis* (syn. *I. ochroleuca*).
11. *Primula sikkimensis.*
12. London Pride = *Saxifraga umbrosa.*
13. Sparganium = *Sparganium ramosum.*
14. Sagittaria = *Sagittaria sagittifolia.*
15. Alisma = *Alisma plantago-aquatica.*
16. Butomus = *Butomus umbellatus.*
17. *Mimulus luteus.*
18. Woodruff = *Asperula odorata.*
19. Lady fern = *Athyrium filix-femina.*

Note: The painting shows a small section of this fan-shaped garden, and the borders slope downwards to the pool. This excludes the following plants from view: Columbine = aquilegia, gentian and *Saxifraga clibrani* [* *S.* × *arendsii* hybrids, 'Carnival', 'Spatlese', 'Triumph': ◇ 'Blood Carpet'].

Below: Jekyll's drawing of Widford tank

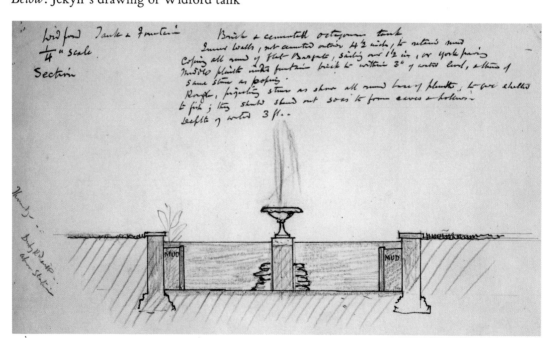

Chapter Eight

Gardens on Different Levels

SUNKEN GARDENS and elegant terraces with stone retaining-walls are an important and distinctive feature of many Jekyll gardens: 'Nothing is prettier or pleasanter than all the various ways of terraced treatment that may be practised with the help of dry-walling... especially where a suitable kind of stone can be found locally' (*Wall and Water Gardens*). In Chapter Six, I have dealt with two dramatic terraced gardens where the hard landscaping is the dominant feature of the gardens. This chapter includes three gardens where the terracing is much gentler and is a subordinate part of the garden's design and planting.

Walsham House is an Edwardian mansion set high in the Surrey hills. The whole estate is about fifty-one acres in size and includes two lodges as well as the main house. The house was formerly owned by Arthur Kenrick who moved here from Field House, Clent, in the early nineteen twenties (see Chapter Seven). Jekyll had produced a successful scheme for the Field House gardens, and Kenrick, no doubt inspired by this, commisssioned her to produce ideas for his new garden. She worked on these over a period of nine years, from 1920 to 1929, and there are still sixty plans of this garden in existence today. This exceeds any other existing number of plans for a single garden, including gardens of the Lutyens/Jekyll partnership.

Jekyll's designs for the Walsham House gardens were a real 'tour de force'. They covered an extraordinarily comprehensive range of features which individually would have added distinction to any garden. There were fine terracing, handsome herbaceous borders, a circular garden and a pergola which covered a long flight of steps leading down to a semi-circular terraced iris garden. This last garden resembled a miniature Greek theatre in its construction with shallow borders replacing the seats. Where the stage would have been at the centre below the tiers, there still stands a delightful summerhouse typical of Jekyll's style. The garden also had a sunken rose garden, rockery and pool, and landscaped woodland with extensive shrubberies of rhododendrons.

I had great difficulty tracking down the location of this house and at one point concluded that it had been demolished. But I had been so attracted by the plans that I felt I had to persevere further. Eventually, after much research, I discovered that the house had changed its name twice on passing into new ownership; thus 'Walsham House' was no longer known in the area. The house had been sold to the Rev. Cyril Cresswell, formerly the Queen's chaplain. He changed its name to Three Barrows Place marking the fact that there are prehistoric tumuli in the estate grounds. In 1974 Cresswell sold the house to its present owner who has again changed its name, which he wishes to keep private.

XXV. Walsham House Herbaceous Terraced Borders

The painting of this garden in Surrey shows that Jekyll had designed the upper terrace of herbaceous borders in a divided colour sequence. The border to the right of the flight of steps, which is flanked by stone boxes of yuccas, is filled with warm-coloured flowering plants

including helenium, helianthus, orange tiger lilies, scarlet monarda and kniphofia. The border on the far side of the steps features the cool purples and blues of aconitum, anchusa, eryngium, nepeta and white hollyhocks, *Chrysanthemum maximum*, dahlias and phlox. Cool colours are repeated in the planting of the lower terraced borders and dry stone wall. A circular garden is shown in the background.

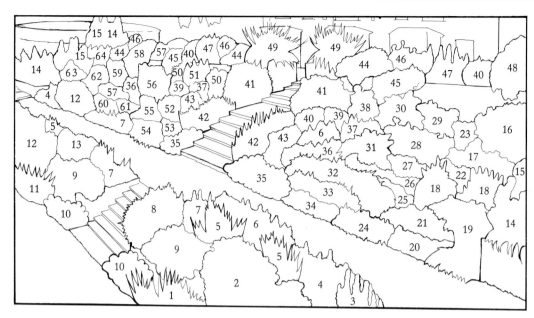

Walsham House Terraced Herbaceous Borders (pages 94–5)

1. Iris = tall bearded iris – 'Queen of May', pink/red self [* 'Rosy Wings', 'Susan Bliss': ◊ 'Playgirl', 'Priceless Pearl', 'Adventuress', 'Pearly Shells', Lace Jabot', soft lilac-pink].
2. *Convolvulus cneorum.*
3. Pink snapdragons.
4. Purple sage = *Salvia officinalis* 'Purpurascens'.
5. Iris [unspecified by Jekyll].
6. White snapdragons.
7. Stachys = *Stachys olympica* (syn *S. byzantina*).
8. Dwarf lavender = *Lavandula angustifolia* 'Hidcote' (syn *L. nana atropurpurea*).
9. Rock pinks.
10. *Megasea ligulata (Bergenia ligulata* or * *B. schmidtii*).
11. Iris = tall bearded iris – 'Darius', blue/yellow bicolour [* 'Golden Alps': ◊ 'Lullaby of Spring', 'Bold Accent', 'Tequila Sunrise', 'Sostenique'].
12. Nepeta = *Nepeta* × *faassenii*.
13. *Eryngium planum.*
14. *Yucca filamentosa.*
15. *Yucca recurvifolia.*
16. *Choisya ternata.*
17. Monarda = *Monarda didyma.*
18. Tritoma (Kniphofia).
19. Montbretia (Crocosmia).
20. Dwarf French marigolds.
21. Orange African marigolds.
22. Tall French marigolds.
23. *Dahlia* 'Fire King' = described as both a scarlet decorative and cactus dahlia. Also named 'Glare of the Garden'.

24. Ophiopogon = *Liriope muscari* or *Ophiopogon spicatum*, a variety no longer available.
25. *Helenium pumilum.*
26. *Buphthalmum salicifolium.*
27. *Oenothera fruticosa.*
28. Tiger lilies = *Lilium tigrinum.*
29. *Helenium striatum (H. autumnale striatum*, gold and crimson [* *H. hoopesii* 'Red and Gold': ◊ *H. autumnale* 'Gartensonne']).
30. *Helianthus* 'Miss Mellish', tall, golden yellow [* *H. atrorubens* 'Monarch', *H. decapetalus* 'Loddon Gold'].
31. Day lily = Hemerocallis.
32. *Glyceria aquatica [G. maxima* 'Variegata'].
33. Calceolaria = *Calceolaria integrifolia.*
34. Variegated mint.
35. Megasea (Bergenia = *Bergenia cordifolia*).
36. Yellow snapdragons.
37. White *Campanula persicifolia (C. persicifolia alba*).
38. White dahlia.
39. Clary = *Salvia sclarea.*
40. *Clematis recta.*
41. Laurustinus *(Viburnum tinus).*
42. Rosemary.
43. *Clematis* 'Davidiana' *(C. heracleifolia* 'Davidiana').
44. Veronica [unspecified. Suggest *Veronica traversii*, now *Hebe brachysiphon*].
45. *Clematis jackmanii.*
46. Echinops = *Echinops ritro.*
47. Acanthus = *Acanthus spinosus.*
48. Fuchsia = *Fuchsia magellanica* 'Gracilis'.
49. *Yucca gloriosa.*

(continued opposite)

Over the years there have been substantial alterations and the introduction of new building to the gardens, but the gardens today still retain the unmistakeable stamp of Jekyll. The site is arranged on a series of different levels marked by retaining walls of Bargate stone. The structure of the tiered semi-circular iris garden with its summerhouse is in good condition, but is now used as a rose garden. This garden is reached by a descent of a hundred steps of original Bargate stone over which there still stands a pergola, but it is not the original structure. The wild garden with its rockery and water feature and winding woodland walks among shrubberies of rhododendrons is still in existence and has a fluency of design which is typical of Jekyll.

The painting shows a part of the gardens as designed by Jekyll in two plans. The first plan is of a double terrace behind the house with steps leading from the upper level, which was probably paved as it is today, to a lower level with generous herbaceous borders designed to give an exuberant summer display of flowers. Interesting features of the design were the large yucca containers, placed at either end of these borders, and the smaller yucca boxes on the upper terrace. Beyond the herbaceous borders was a circular garden reached by steps from the upper terrace. This plan was produced by Jekyll in November 1920.

A second plan produced in August 1924 incorporated the first plan and suggested a third level with a dry stone wall and a set of steps which lined up with the original flight leading down from the upper terrace. A grass walk divided the herbaceous borders from a narrow border running along the top of the dry stone wall. There is a suggestion on this later plan that the herbaceous border was lengthened to include some shrub planting and either a second yucca box was introduced or perhaps the original one at the end of the border was moved. I have shown the upper terraces as they appear in the 1920 plan with just a section of the lower terrace in the picture. The garden is shown in August.

Although these herbaceous borders are divided by steps, Jekyll has still kept to her principle of cool flower colours leading into warm yellows, oranges and reds. In this design, however, she has produced a cool border and a warm border. I have reversed my usual viewpoint of looking at Jekyll's borders from the cool end and have shown the warm colours in the foreground. An enclosed yucca bed planted out with *Yucca recurvifolia* and *Yucca filamentosa* is just in the picture. Immediately behind it is a mass of crocosmia and dwarf French marigolds with a drift of taller African marigolds ranged behind them. The torches of kniphofia stand out among the other plants with yet

50. *Dahlia* 'Henry Patrick', described as both a white decorative or cactus dahlia.
51. White hollyhocks.
52. *Aconitum japonicum*, pale blue [* *A. wilsonii*: ◊ *A. carmichaelii*], *Chrysanthemum maximum*, *Asphodelus ramosus*.
53. *Campanula carpatica*.
54. White pinks.
55. *Aster acris* and polemonium = *Polemonium caeruleum*.
56. *Phlox* 'Avalanche', white [* 'White Admiral,

'Rembrandt': ◊ 'Mt. Fuji], clary = *Salvia sclarea*, *Echinops ritro*, *Artemisia lactiflora*.
57. *Eryngium* × *oliverianum*.
58. White everlasting pea = *Lathyrus latifolius albus*.
59. Delphinium, *Aster umbellatus*, anchusa.
60. China aster 'Victoria Blue'.
61. Dicentra = *Dicentra eximia*.
62. Purple dahlia and erigeron.
63. *Eryngium giganteum*.
64. Vine = vitis.

another swathe of marigolds weaving between their clumps of rush-like leaves.

Jekyll seems to have made a particular feature of the type of foliage in the plan for this border. There are the strappy leaves of crocosmia and hemerocallis, the sword-like foliage of the yuccas, and the softer leaves of her favourite *Glyceria aquatica*: 'Though this is a plant whose proper place is in wet ground, it will accomodate itself to the flower border' (*Colour in the Flower Garden*). I have shown the variegated form which she commonly used. At the front of the border there is also a planting of ophiopogon and I have taken this to be *Ophiopogon graminifolius* (now known as *Liriope muscari*), a late-flowering plant with spikes of small purple bells. These were planted in between the dwarf French marigolds and a drift of variegated mint which was followed by a clump of bergenia planted next to the central flight of steps. The steps were flanked on either side with rosemary and *Viburnum tinus*.

The warm colour scheme of this border is sustained by a variety of flowers, and different shapes of petals and blooms add texture and interest to the border: the tousled red heads of monarda and the scarlet *Dahlia* 'Fire King', tall deep gold 'Miss Mellish', a variety of helianthus which is no longer available, and *Helenium striatum*, a variety described in one old gardening book as being crimson and gold. Tall tiger lilies with their orange-red recurved petals stand next to a clump of hemerocallis and are surrounded by yellow and white snapdragons and golden *Helenium pumilum* and buphthalmum. The yellow purses of calceolaria add a new flower shape to the border. Cool white *Campanula persicifolia*, a white dahlia and the hyacinth-like blue flowers of *Clematis heracleifolia* 'Davidiana' emphasize the warmth of the other flower colours. Over the top of the wall, planted in the border on the top terrace, can be seen the steel-blue heads of echinops and an architectural acanthus. *Clematis* 'Jackmanii' tumbles over the wall.

The cool border has a typical front row of Jekyll favourites: bergenia, white pinks and stachys followed by nepeta and velvety purple sage. Behind these are *Eryngium giganteum* and *Eryngium* x *oliverianum*, *Aster acris*, *Campanula carpatica* and blue China asters. The other blues include anchusa, echinops and light blue *Aconitum japonicum*. White flowers bring out the cool clarity of the blues. There are white hollyhocks and phlox, a white tree lupin, *Chrysanthemum maximum* and the tall *Dahlia* 'Henry Patrick'. Drifts of yellow and white snapdragons weave in between the other plants. At the end of the border, the yuccas, contained in their own enclosure, give architectural form to the border. The two *Yucca gloriosa* planted in the yucca boxes on either side of the top of the steps dominate these lower borders. Jekyll gave instructions for the construction of the boxes: 'Coping about 22", wall 2" thick... walling may be rough inside'. Once again, plants from the top terrace border can be seen over the wall.

The lower border and dry stone wall are planted with a cool colour scheme leading into warmer colours which are just out of this picture. *Convolvulus cneorum* is in the foreground separated by the spikes of iris from a clump of purple sage. Beyond are white snapdragons, stachys and dwarf lavender. Rock pinks fall in a mass over the wall. A generous drift of nepeta contrasts with a more disciplined clump of *Eryngium planum* nearby.

XXVI. Stonepitts Terraced Garden

A typical Jekyll colour scheme of blue and pink flowers complemented by silver and grey foliage, designed for a manor house garden in Kent in 1925.

The second terraced garden I have shown is in Kent. Stonepitts is a fine old brick manor house, mostly dating from the seventeenth century with some older parts. It commands views over a wide valley. The site is partly terraced into several levels and extends to about eleven acres. The house was acquired in 1925 by Lady Rhonda and Mrs. Helen Archdale. A letter to Jekyll dated 25 May 1925 records an interesting link between Stonepitts and nearby Chart Cottage (see Chapter Four): 'Lady Rhonda and I have been for four years in pleasant enjoyment of a garden laid out by yourself for Mr. Blunt, at Chart Cottage, Seal Sevenoaks. The owner is refusing a renewal of the lease and we have to move, but only a few hundred yards'. Helen Archdale wrote copiously to Jekyll providing her with detailed information about the site for the gardens at Stonepitts; one letter is fifteen pages long.

The present garden still retains the terracing, walls and steps of the garden as planned by Jekyll. Some features, particularly the layout of hard landscaping at the back of the house, appear to be slightly different from her plans but, on the whole, the bones of the garden are still there. There are mature trees in the grounds; many of these are probably original, including the magnificent lime at the front of the house. The back of the building looks out on a paved courtyard with a well, sheltered by a canopy of ancient wisteria. Steps lead up to wrought iron gates and then up a path which cuts across a lawn.

The path leads to the second level of the garden where successive flights of steps, and paths in between, allow one to walk to the far end of the gardens. Each level is separated from the next by a terrace wall. At the junction of wall and steps where a new level is reached, there are handsome Irish yews. These are old and could certainly date back to 1925 when Jekyll designed the garden but, as they are not marked on her plans, perhaps they were put in as alternatives to her planting. They now dominate the series of terraces.

The other side of the house is flanked by oast houses which the Archdales had once hoped to convert into guest houses. There is a small grassed courtyard beyond the oast house and behind this is an informal part of the garden. The landscaping is full of curved shapes in contrast to the geometric structure of the terraces, and part of this informal area is laid out as a rockery. At a lower level, there is a pool and stream, now choked with weeds, which was the subject of a lengthy correspondence, including sketches, from Helen Archdale to Jekyll. Ten plans remain of Jekyll's scheme for the gardens.

Helen Archdale, one of the co-owners of Stonepitts Manor, must have been, at least in one respect, an ideal client for she provided Jekyll with pages of detailed descriptions, photographs and little sketches of her garden. This enables a clear picture of the site in its previous state to be formed in one's mind. She tried to persuade Jekyll to visit the garden and spend the night 'or nights or if one day was all, to make any meal at your convenience'. But Jekyll treated her like other clients who lived at a distance; she declined the invitation but suggested that Mrs. Archdale might like to visit Munstead Wood instead, for 'an hour's discussion will save a good deal of correspondence on both sides'.

The painting shows part of the main flower borders. This part of the garden was at the back of the house and Lady Rhonda and Mrs. Archdale 'saw terraced paved gardens rising up this slope with perhaps a broad series of steps'. Jekyll was obviously inspired by the idea and wrote: 'It is a great opportunity for a fine effort from that piece of rising ground' and she suggested that 'I can supply plants a good deal to your advantage both as to price and strength'. The colour scheme she proposed was to be subtly varied with each terrace beginning nearest the house with a predominance of yellow. Then, on the next terrace, red mixed in with the yellow followed by a scheme of blue and pink. White flowers were used on all the terraces and this gave freshness and a sense of visual continuity to Jekyll's design.

My painting shows the blue and pink terrace in June. Beyond this, a flight of steps leads up to a lawn which has a paved alcove with a seat sheltered by thick yew hedging. Curved borders on either side of the steps are planted generously with lavender and edged with *Stachys olympica*. Stachys edges the path on the terrace below, punctuated by white pinks and *Sedum spectabile* and bergenia nearest the steps. Pale blue tradescantia and deeper blue nepeta flank the path in the foreground where steps drop to a lower terrace. On the left side, *Aster acris* and purple sage is followed by pink snapdragons, *Chrysanthemum maximum* and *Geranium ibericum*. Beyond the nepeta in the right border is a generous clump of *Chrysanthemum maximum* and behind it there are drifts of santolina, *Aster acris*, *Filipendula rubra* and tradescantia. The delicacy of the colour scheme is characteristic of Jekyll and depends as much on her subtle deployment of foliage tones and textures as on her fresh use of flower colours.

My final garden in this chapter is a near neighbour to Jekyll's own house and garden at Munstead Wood. Stilemans was originally part of a large estate but even today it still comprises sixteen acres of gardens. The house was built for Dr. Edward Arnold by the architect Sir Charles Nicholson in about 1908. The garden was designed by Jekyll in two stages beginning in 1909; twenty-five plans remain from this period. Dr. Arnold who had been out in India had the house built, possibly for his retirement or periodic returns from the Far East. Sadly, he never lived long enough to enjoy his new house, as he died of blood poisoning shortly after beginning his new life there. The house was eventually bought by a Mrs. Dearden who was able, as an elderly lady, to provide the present owner with its history and photographs of the house and grounds in their prime. Stilemans, in its day, was thought sufficiently distinctive to warrant a feature in a 1937 edition of the magazine, *Country Life*.

The house is a handsome cream stone mansion which occupies a flat plateau of land above Godalming. Of the original garden, there remain many groups of trees that appear on Jekyll's plans and an attractively landscaped area of light woodland underplanted with azaleas. The formal features of the garden defined by dense yew hedges are also still in existence. These include an elegant yew-hedged walk and an enclosed peony garden, now planted with roses, and a sunken garden.

The sunken garden at Stilemans has its counterparts in many Jekyll gardens. Its layout is classic of its kind and period: three different levels of planting achieve considerable visual interest. At the lowest level is a central area of lawn formally laid out with a long rectangular Italianate pool, a shape and design which Jekyll probably saw repeated in many Italian gardens during her visits to Europe earlier in her life. Within the surrounding rectangle of lawn there are decoratively scalloped borders designed to be used for annual bedding, and there is also an indication of some formally-shaped trees or, perhaps, topiary features. The present owner of Stilemans told me that there had been some small trees within this area but did not know whether these were planted at Jekyll's time or afterwards. Jekyll's plan only marked the borders with the word 'Snap' but we can gather from this that she was suggesting a formal bedding of snapdragons. She did not specify a colour so I have suggested one of her favourites, 'tall Snapdragons palest yellow, half-way between yellow and white', as this would have fitted in with the prevailing colour scheme of the rest of the garden.

The central lawn is enclosed by low dry-stone walls of the local Bargate stone.

XXVII. Stilemans Sunken Garden

The formal layout of this sunken garden in Surrey was classic of its kind. A central lawn was enclosed by terracing. The painting takes an angled view of the garden with a rectangular Italianate pool shown diagonally across the left-hand corner of the picture. In the right-hand

corner, part of a decorative scalloped bed of snapdragons can be seen. Shallow stone steps are flanked by *Rhododendron myrtifolium*. The wall on either side is planted with rock plants which also cover the surface of the wall on the next level up. The borders above are planted with roses in yellows, apricot, pink and red and varieties of grey-leaved plants.

Stilemans Sunken Garden (pages 102–3)

1. Red water lilies = *Nymphaea* 'Laydekeri Fulgens'.
2. Pink water lilies = *Nymphaea* 'Marliacea Rosea'.
3. White water lilies = *Nymphaea* 'Marliacea Albida'.
4. 'Chromatella' = *Nymphaea* 'Marliacea Chromatella'.
5. Snapdragons.
6. Rose helianthemum.
7. *Phlox amoena (P. × procumbens).*
8. *Scabiosa pterocephala (Pterocephalus perennis perennis).*
9. Nepeta = *Nepeta × faassenii.*
10. White thrift = *Armeria maritima* 'Alba'.
11. *Rhododendron myrtifolium.*
12. Erinus = *Erinus alpinus.*
13. *Saxifraga sancta (Saxifraga juniperifolia).*
14. Yellow helianthemum.
15. *Campanula garganica.*
16. Valerian = *Centranthus ruber.*
17. *Sedum spurium.*
18. *Veronica rupestris (V. prostrata).*
19. Rock pinks.
20. *Othonnopsis cheirifolia* (syn. *Othonna cheirifolia).*
21. *Plumbago larpentae (Ceratostigma plumbaginoides).*
22. Aubretia.
23. Cerastium.

24. *Campanula elatines.*
25. Rose 'Mme Ravary' (HT), orange/yellow [* 'Sutter's Gold'].
26. Rose 'Mme Melanie Soupert' (Tea), orange/yellow [* 'Golden Melody'].
27. Rose 'Miss Alice de Rothschild' (Tea), gold/lemon [* 'Cynthia Brooke'].
28. Rose 'Lady Hillingdon' (HT).
29. Rose 'Sunburst' (HT), yellow [* 'Joanna Hill'].
30. Lavender = *Lavandula angustifolia.*
31. Santolina = *Santolina chamaecyparissus.*
32. Stachys = *Stachys olympica (syn. S. byzantina).*
33. Rose 'Richmond' (HT), scarlet-red [* 'Hugh Dickson'].
34. Rose 'General MacArthur' (HT), rose-red [* 'Mister Lincoln'].
35. Rose 'Mrs. Edward Powell' (HT), crimson [* 'Francois Dubreuil': ◊ 'Crimson Glory'].
36. Rose 'Lady Pirrie' (HT), salmon/apricot [* 'Angèle Pernet'].
37. Rose 'Joseph Hill' (HT), salmon/yellow [* 'Barbara Richards': ◊ 'Confidence'].
38. Rose 'Harry Kirk' (Tea), yellow [* 'Perle des Jardins'].
39. Rose 'George C. Waud' (HT), vermilion [* 'Blessings' or 'Mischief': ◊ 'Tropicana'].

[*Note: I have suggested alternatives for 'Richmond' and 'General MacArthur' because today these roses are only available as climbers.]

Shallow steps lead up to the next level of the garden, a grass walk with another dry-stone wall on one side joining this level with the third and highest section of the garden. The steps on either side of the lawn are flanked by borders planted with *Rhododendron myrtifolium*. The present owner can remember plantings of rhododendron in these borders but recalls that these areas became water-logged and, since the plants looked extremely unhappy, they were removed. The rectangular pool was once defined by stone coping and there was also originally an indication of some central feature, possibly a statue or fountain. Jekyll suggests six groups of water lilies for the pool: at one end, a red and two pink and at the other end, two white groups and — the only specified variety — the yellow 'Chromatella'. I have examined the lists of water lilies recommended by Jekyll in *Wall and Water Gardens* and have chosen for the white water lilies *Nymphaea* 'Marliacea Albida', for the pink *Nymphaea* 'Marliacea Rosea', and for the red *Nymphaea* 'Laydekeri Fulgens'.

The low dry-stone walls enclosing the garden at two levels are liberally planted with rock plants which spill exuberantly over the honey-coloured stone in a mixture of soft pastel colours. These introduce an informality into the planting scheme making a marked contrast with the geometry of the central lawn and pool. Jekyll used some old cottage garden favourites for this planting as well as some rarer alpines. Helianthemum in rose pink and yellow, armeria, campanula, aubretia, cerastium and rock pinks are mixed with varieties of saxifrage including the evergreen *Saxifraga juniperifolia*. A charming little rock scabious which combines pink flower heads with grey leaves, *Pterocephalus perennis perennis*, adds to a theme of grey foliage already represented in generous groups of lavender, nepeta, santolina and stachys which are planted at the top of the wall on the third level.

This is a garden which combines three elements in one design — a formal pool garden, a dry-stone wall garden and finally, a rose garden. The top level is a long border with a double layer of roses backed and set off to advantage by dense yew hedging. This hedge is still in a splendid state of preservation today and many of the planting of stachys, nepeta and lavender marked on Jekyll's plan of this level are, although not the original plants, still present in this border.

The colour scheme of the rose bed is an interesting one. Jekyll used positive reds and pinks for the back row of roses and a mixture of warm yellows and apricots for the front row. The occasional introduction of a sharper yellow rose brings out the warmer tones of the other roses. The back row is made up of hybrid tea roses: 'Richmond', a pure scarlet red rose; 'General MacArthur', a deep rosy red; 'Mrs. Edward Powell', velvety crimson; 'George C. Waud', cochineal crimson. The front row combines in sequence: 'Mme. Ravary', orange yellow; 'Mme. Melanie Soupert', orange and yellow blooms with a cupped form; 'Miss Alice de Rothschild', a golden and lemon yellow tea rose; 'Lady Hillingdon', a deep apricot yellow hybrid tea; 'Sunburst', yellow bloom with orange yellow centre; 'Lady Pirrie', coppery salmon outside with the inside of the bloom, apricot yellow; 'Joseph Hill', salmon pink shaded with yellow; 'Harry Kirk', a deep sulphur yellow tea rose.

I have illustrated this garden in June when the roses would have been at their best and I have taken a long view from a high perspective so that the majority of the planting can be seen.

Chapter Nine

Dry Wall and Rock Gardens

F EW OF THE MANY GARDEN PICTURES which Jekyll created through her planting have as much charm as those where tumbling masses of rock plants cover the surfaces of mellow brick or stone. Her ideas were conceived as a result of observation; she had seen rock plants growing among stones in the Mediterranean area and English wild flowers colonising a wall and had observed how these plants could thrive given the protection of a crevice between the stones or bricks.

The small painting shows a section of classic Jekyll dry-stone wall planting planned for a site near the kitchen garden of Stilemans (see Chapter Eight). I have shown it in late June. The wall was constructed to lean slightly backwards, 'so that no drop of rain is lost, but all runs into the joints', and to descend in three steps so that there were three levels or heights. The material used was, almost certainly, Bargate stone, in keeping with walls elsewhere in the garden.

Two groups of dwarf lavender at the top of the wall are separated, on the left of the picture, by *Sisyrinchium striatum*. The glaucous spoon-shaped leaves and bright yellow flowers of *Othonna cheirifolia* (syn. *Othonnopsis cheirifolia*) tumble over the wall on the right. These two plants, with their distinctive structured form and foliage, contrast with the soft masses of blooms covering the wall below: rock pinks, white cerastium and creamy double arabis. Nepeta, planted in the wall on the left, repeats the blue tones of the lavender above and a patch of *Sedum spurium*, on the right, is the only plant not in flower. *Iris unguicularis* is planted at the foot of the wall.

Jekyll's plans for her clients often suggested transforming natural slopes and dells in a garden into rock gardens. These could be on a grand or modest scale, but were landscaped with paths in between the rocky outcrops which were covered with shrubs and lower-growing rock plants and alpines. Water in the form of a stream, natural pool or bog-garden was introduced, where possible, as a special feature: 'Where water is available, and especially where there is a natural supply and a good fall in the ground level, the delights of the rock-garden may be greatly increased. Nothing is more interesting than to plan and construct a combination of rock and water' (*Wall, Water and Woodland Gardens*). Jekyll was able to combine these two elements in her design for a Norfolk garden.

Drayton Wood, near Norwich, Norfolk, was once privately owned but is now a small country house hotel. The building dates from 1906 and Jekyll was commissioned in 1921 by Lt. Col. O'Meara, a retired Indian Army officer, to produce a scheme for the one and a half acres of gardens, set among nine acres of woodland. This setting must have appealed to Jekyll as woodland surroundings were a feature of her own gardens at Munstead Wood. Nine plans remain of her original scheme.

XXVIII. Drayton Wood Rock and Pool Garden

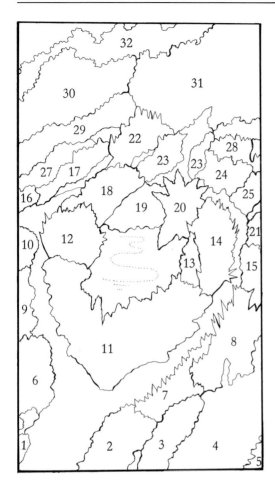

7. *Plumbago larpentae (Ceratostigma plumbaginoides)*.
8. *Sisyrinchium bermudiana*.
9. *Aubrieta*.
10. *Campanula carpatica*.
11. *Struthiopteris germanica (Matteuccia struthiopteris*, the ostrich feather fern).
12. *Iris sibirica*.
13. Mimulus = *Mimulus cupreus*
14. *Iris orientalis* (syn. *I. ochroleuca*).
15. Rock pinks.
16. *Polygonum bunonsis (P. affine)*.
17. *Silene alpestris*.
18. *Spiraea ulmaria (Filipendula ulmaria)*.
19. *Senecio clivorum (Ligularia dentata)*.
20. Lady fern = *Athyrium filix-femina*.
21. Mossy saxifrage = *Saxifraga burseriana*.
22. Tiarella = *Tiarella cordifolia*.
23. Iberis = *Iberis sempervirens*.
24. Saxifraga = *Saxifraga longifolia*.
25. *Phlox stellaria* [* P. 'G. F. Wilson'].
26. Ophiopogon = *Liriope muscari* or *Ophiopogon spicatum*, a variety no longer available.
27. Lithospermum = *Lithospermum diffusum* (syn. *Lithodora diffusa*).
28. *Omphalodes verna*.
29. *Andromeda axillaris (Leucothoë axillaris)*.
30. *Rhododendron myrtifolium*.
31. *Rhododendron ferrugineum*.
32. *Rhus cotinus (Cotinus coggygria)*.

Drayton Wood Rock and Pool Garden (page 107)

1. Cerastium.
2. Helianthemum.
3. *Scabiosa pterocephala (Pterocephalus perennis perennis)*.
4. Purple sage = *Salvia officinalis* 'Purpurascens.
5. White thrift = *Armeria maritima* 'Alba'.
6. *Sedum spurium*.

The fate of Drayton Wood has followed the pattern of so many Jekyll gardens. The house passed out of private hands and eventually was acquired by the local authority to be turned into a retirement home. Although during this period the gardens underwent some changes, they were not appreciably altered. The present owners were alerted to the fact that they possessed a Jekyll garden by a member of the staff of Durham

University. As a result they now have an ambitious plan to restore the gardens according to Jekyll's original designs, combining this long-term project with alterations and improvements to the hotel itself. Jekyll only designed one other garden in Norfolk so that the Drayton Wood gardens, once they are planted and have matured, will be of special interest.

Jekyll's plans for Drayton Wood show some formal gardens but the main feature of her design was a network of paths looping round areas richly planted out with shrubs. The pathways link the formal gardens to surrounding woodland so that there is a natural progression from one area to the other, providing a sense of harmony and cohesion to the overall design of the site.

Set among this informal network of paths is a rock garden with, as its central focus, a small irregularly shaped pool. I have chosen this as the subject for my painting and I have shown it in June. The pool is fringed with ferns; meadow sweet (*Filipendula ulmaria*) and *Ligularia dentata* are planted at one end and on either side, facing each other, are groups of *Iris sibirica* and *Iris orientalis* (syn. *I. ochroleuca*). A bright little mimulus is planted right at the water's edge so that its yellow flowers would be reflected in the water.

Jekyll produced a detailed drawing for the landscaping of this area and she also included instructions for the making of the pool: 'The border marked 3″ all round tank to be only just even with the water line at the bottom or a trifle below, so that it is always damp and boggy'. Her planting plan for the surrounding rockery came with a sketch showing the layout of stones for the garden, '200 lumps of stone, long shapes', and she refers her client to Chapter Two of her book on *Wall and Water Gardens* featuring the rock garden construction she had in mind: 'It is far better to set the stones more or less in lines of stratification, just as we see them in nature in a stone quarry or any mountain side where surface denudation has left them standing out in nearly parallel lines. It matters not the least whether the courses are far apart or near together; this is naturally settled by the steepness of the ground'. In this case the slopes were gradual and the whole garden was protected by an outer cordon of shrubs. In the painting *Rhododendron myrtifolium* and *Rhododendron ferrugineum* are shown at one end of the garden with *Leucothoë axillaris* planted in front of these shrubs; *Cotinus coggygria* stands behind.

The rock garden plants chosen for this garden are a familiar Jekyll selection and the colour scheme with its lack of brashness, combining blue, cream and soft pink with an occasional touch of yellow, is an example of her unfailingly subtle palette. There is blue aubrieta, campanula, intenser blue lithodora and the star shaped flowers of *Sisyrinchium bermudianum* set amongst their spiky leaves. A mass of rock pinks fall over the stones in the right of the picture and richer pink *Sedum spurium* forms a dense mat of colour in one corner. I have shown a pink helianthemum in the foreground but, as Jekyll does not specify a colour for this rock rose, it is possible that a yellow or white variety was intended for this position. In the background the blooms of rhododendrons add yet another tone of pink. Frothy cream heads of meadow sweet overlook the pool and behind them stand the erect spikes of *Tiarella cordifolia*. Nearby, white *Silene alpestris* clings close to the rocks forming a mat of tiny flowers and, on the right of the painting, *Saxifraga longifolia* erects its impressive panicles 'of creamy white flower sometimes two

XXIX. A detail of dry wall planting at Stilemans

A classic example of Jekyll's dry wall planting. Lavender and sisyrinchium are planted on top of the wall; tumbling masses of rock plants cover its surface.

feet long'. In the foreground, velvety textured purple sage grows above *Pterocephalus perennis perennis*, the delightful little woolly-leaved scabious: 'The neat little Scabiosa Pterocephala must have a place'. Separating these two plants there should be a drift of a plant whose identity eludes the decipherment of Jekyll's handwriting on the plan. Reluctantly, therefore, I have had to leave it out of the scheme.

Chapter Ten

The Rose Garden

'ONE OF THE MANY WAYS in which the splendid enthusiasm for good gardening – an enthusiasm which only grows stronger as time goes on – is showing itself, is in the general desire to use beautiful Roses more worthily' (*Roses For English Gardens*). During her lifetime Jekyll encouraged a new and more creative approach to using roses in the garden. She departed from the traditionally accepted view that they were best displayed in a formal arrangement and maintained that roses could be used in limitless ways which were not usually considered by conventional gardeners of her day. Her artist's need for innovation and her ability to combine plants and colours inspired her to devise new uses for a wide variety of roses and to mix them together with other plants. Jekyll's informal use of roses is one of her valuable legacies to modern gardeners.

The paintings in this book show many examples of the different ways in which she combined roses with other plants and selected the colours of their blooms to create a harmonious garden picture. In the sunken garden at Rignall Wood (see Chapter Three) she planted her favourite China roses among rosemary and lavender, choosing a soft blue, pink and grey colour scheme to complement the delicate colours of the roses. The pergola which forms part of the same garden was planted with climbers and ramblers to add variety among the other climbing plants. She also loved to cover the wall of a house or to festoon arches or bowers with a rich display of roses. On the steeply sloping banks of the Ohio garden, Elmhurst (see Chapter Six), she planted ramblers to grow in 'free fountain shape without any artificial support... with trees and bushes in shrub clumps' between garden and woodland so that the formal part of the garden blended into the wilder area beyond. She planted roses to cascade over a terraced wall at Elmhurst and in the second garden in this chapter, at Henley Park, her favourite 'Jersey Beauty' is used as ground cover to carpet a bank. She also used climbers and ramblers to camouflage unsightly objects like an old tree or an unattractive building in the garden.

Contemporary gardeners, however, still wanted Jekyll to design formal rose gardens with geometrically arranged beds and massed displays of roses, although she had admitted her lack of enthusiasm for 'the usual Rose garden, generally a sort of target of concentric rings of beds placed upon turf, often with no special aim at connected design with the portions of the garden immediately about it, and filled with plants without a thought of their colour effect or any other worthy intention' (*Roses for English Gardens*).

The rose gardens I have painted still retain a traditional form of geometric layout with complexes of L-shaped beds which make up into squares; but Jekyll's sensitive use of colour gives them a distinction. Her knowledge of bedding roses appears to have been limited and she relied on the advice of Edward Mawley, her co-author of *Roses for English Gardens*. It may be that she was simply less interested in formal rose bedding than other aspects of garden design and found it too limiting for her personal taste.

The point has been made to me by an authority on roses that Jekyll used what would have been regarded at the time as 'modern' varieties instead of established older roses which had been proved to be reliable. A case in point was her use of the hybrid tea, 'Killarney'. H.H. Thomas in his *Complete Gardener* (1912) said: 'The one great fault of this rose is that it is sadly addicted to mildew'. Jekyll had obviously chosen 'Killarney' for its attractive form and colour and had not discovered its lack of resistance to disease. Perhaps this is why so many of the bedding roses which she used have subsequently been abandoned by rose breeders in favour of varieties of hybrid teas which are more disease resistant. Conversely, many of the fine old roses which Jekyll used, and which predate her period of design, feature in current rose lists and are still chosen for today's gardens.

Jekyll imaginatively compensated for the limitations imposed on her by the layout of traditional rose gardens by introducing some new element into their design. She commented that 'a Rose garden may often be made much more delightful by having some one point of interest besides the Roses' because otherwise the rose garden would become 'a dull place'. Her critical view of rose gardens may account for the sites they occupy on her plans. She often sited her rose gardens in a hedged enclosure away from the house and its windows. Although the hedging was planned to protect the roses against wind or frost, it may also have been designed to hide the rose garden from view. Perhaps Jekyll felt that roses did not provide as much year-round interest as other arrangements of plants: during the winter, their bare and thorny bushes could present a depressing picture.

In the first of the two rose gardens in this chapter, Jekyll adds a water lily pool to enliven the garden's design. The second garden has its setting as its 'point of interest'. This is a sunken rose garden with a large formal bedding display recessed among banks of flowering shrubs and plants which were mixed with species roses. Here Jekyll has been able to combine the traditional formal rose garden with her favourite informal use of roses.

The rose garden at Field House, Clent, was one of the designs which Jekyll produced for Arthur Kenrick through his architects, Forbes & Tait (see Chapter Seven). The site of the original rose garden cannot be found today and this may mean that it was never implemented, although the garden was planned to fit into an existing enclosure, surrounded by yew hedging. This, at least, should be traceable if it had not been removed or, perhaps, turned into some of the topiary features which made the gardens of Field House well known locally. The original rose garden was sited a long way from the house and would have required quite a trek across the rest of the grounds to reach it. It was designed with a grouping of formal L-shaped beds surrounding the rectangular lily pool. The whole garden was paved and hedged on two sides. The site was square and, apart from the central complex of beds, there were rose beds on all sides of the paved area with an entrance into the garden through one of the yew hedges. Two of the remaining sides were intended to be open to the rest of the garden. I have taken an angled, high-level view of the planting and have shown the garden in June when the roses would have made their finest display.

The design was achieved by using mainly hybrid tea roses, some of which are still familiar to us today but others are no longer available from modern rose breeders. The central beds of roses created a subtle colour scheme of pinks in different tones and strengths and for these borders Jekyll used two roses which are still available today, 'Mme. Abel Chatenay' and 'Lyon Rose'. The others which formed the groups are now no longer grown and for these I have suggested alternatives. The original roses were 'Mme. Segond Weber', which one contemporary rose book described as a 'bright salmon rose', 'Radiance' described as a 'carmine-salmon', 'Prince de Bulgarie' described as a 'flower silvery flesh, deeper in the centre, delicately shaded with salmon and pale rose' and finally 'Killarney', which was described as a 'flower flesh shaded white, suffused pale pink' (*The Rose Encyclopaedia*, T. Geoffrey and W. Henslow).

The outer borders of roses have a colour scheme made up of a greater variety of colours with several familiar breeds of rose included in the design. 'Hugh Dickson' and 'Mme. Caroline Testout' represent the pinks and 'Frau Karl Druschki' the whites. Other roses in the design are the pink 'Ulrich Brunner Fils', 'Pharisaer', which is a white rose tinted with a delicate pink, 'General MacArthur', a fine rosy red bloom, and the beautiful deep velvety red 'Chateau de Clos Vougeot'. Of these roses, only 'Pharisaer', 'Ulrich Brunner Fils' and 'Frau Karl Druschki' are still grown as bush roses; the others are only available as climbers.

Untraceable varieties among current lists are 'Lieutenant Chauré', a crimson-red, and 'Gruss an Sangerhausen', scarlet. I found this last rose a rather puzzling introduction into the general colour scheme but perhaps Jekyll felt its warmth and brightness enhanced the beauty of the pink roses. 'La Tosca' was a pale silvery pink rose and the three other pale roses in these outer borders were amber white 'Mrs. David McKee', flushed white 'British Queen' and the delicate eau-de-nil white, 'Mrs. Molly Sharman Crawford'. 'Leuchtfeuer' and 'George C. Waud' were both red roses and 'Lady Ashtown' was a free-flowering rose of pure deep pink. All the beds were edged with Jekyll's favourite *Stachys olympica*: 'This edging is not only most becoming to the Roses, but serves a useful purpose by defining the form of the design' (*A Gardener's Testament*).

Jekyll produced her plans for my second garden, Henley Park, in 1909 and today twenty-one drawings still exist of her original scheme for her client, Mrs. Reade Revill. Henley Park, a handsome late Georgian house, was originally the dower house to Fawley Court, a grand establishment by the river situated close to Henley on Thames. I confess that I had a personal reason for wanting to include this garden in my book. I used regularly to pass the curved drive leading to the front door of Henley Park on one of my favourite walks across a stretch of parkland leading to the house and gardens with their enviable position high up on this ridge of the Chilterns.

Unfortunately, after the Second World War the Fawley Court estate was split up and sold off as separate lots and Henley Park became a casualty of this arrangement. The house was left unoccupied for a long period and then was rented out to various tenants. Their lack of commitment to the house and gardens resulted in a neglect of the grounds

XXX. Field House Rose Garden and Water Lily Pool

The layout of this formal rose garden in Worcestershire was typical of many designed by Jekyll. L-shaped beds form a square surrounding a rectangular water lily pool which is a central feature of the garden. The borders round the paved area are also planted with roses. In the

background of the painting, an entrance to the garden is shown through thick yew hedging. The L-shaped beds provide a subtle colour scheme of soft pink hybrid tea roses while, in the outer beds, there is a greater variety of colours ranging from white to deepest pink and bright red. All the beds are edged with the soft grey foliage of *Stachys olympica*.

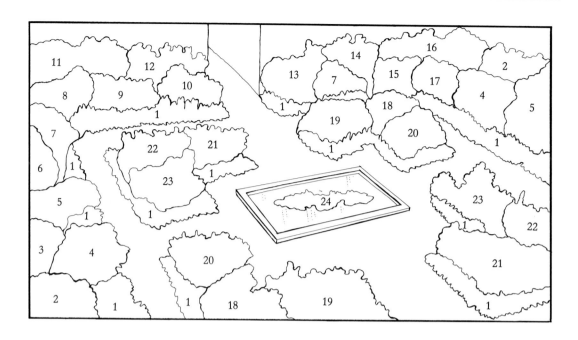

Field House Rose Garden (pages 114–15)

1. Stachys = *Stachys olympica* (syn. *S. byzantina*).
2. 'Mme Caroline Testout' (HT), pink [* 'Home Sweet Home'].
3. 'General MacArthur' (HT), rose-red [* 'Mister Lincoln'].
4. 'Chateau de Clos Vougeot' (HT), velvety red [* 'General Jacqueminot'].
5. 'Lieutenant Chauré' (HT), crimson [* 'Crimson Glory'].
6. 'La Tosca' (HT), silvery pink [* 'Silver Lining'].
7. 'Lady Ashtown' (HT), deep pink [* 'Dame Edith Helen: ◊ 'Tiffany'].
8. 'British Queen' (HT), flushed white [* 'Pascali'].
9. 'Pharisaer' (HT).
10. 'Molly Sharman Crawford' (HT), eau de nil-white [* 'Polar Star'].
11. 'Ulrich Brunner Fils' (HT).
12. 'George C. Waud' (HT), vermilion [* 'Blessings', 'Mischief': ◊ 'Tropicana'].
13. 'Mrs. David McKee' (HT), amber-white [* 'Grace Darling'].
14. 'Leuchtfeuer' (China), red [* 'Cramoisi Superieur'].
15. 'Frau Karl Druschki' (HT).
16. 'Hugh Dickson' (HT).
17. 'Gruss an Sangerhausen' (HT), scarlet [* 'Fragrant Cloud': ◊ 'Carrousel'].
18. 'Mme. Abel Chatenay' (HT).
19. 'Killarney' (HT), blush [* 'Ophelia'].
20. 'Lyon Rose' (HT).
21. 'Mme Segond Weber' (HT), salmon/rose [* 'Antoine Rivoire': ◊ 'Michelle Meilland'].
22. 'Radiance' (HT), carmine-salmon [* 'Mischief': ◊ 'Electron'].
23. 'Prince de Bulgarie' (HT), silvery flesh [* 'Lady Sylvia': ◊ 'Maybelle Stearns'].
24. Water lilies.

[*Note: I have suggested alternatives for 'Mme. Caroline Testout', 'Chateau de Clos Vougeot' and 'General MacArthur', because today these roses are only available as climbers and not as bush roses.]

which might not have occurred under single ownership.

The present owners of Henley Park showed me some original photographs of the grounds which must have been taken when the gardens were in their prime. The photographs showed generous herbaceous borders, characteristic of Jekyll's planting and style, flanking either side of a grass walk. The planting plan for these borders is no longer in existence. Vestiges of Jekyll's original garden still remain in the form of some massive yew hedging which has reverted in one or two places so that the hedge is now punctuated by fully grown yew trees. Two fine old acers correspond with a plan that Jekyll produced for mixed borders of shrubs and perennials, and a tennis lawn, a common feature of gardens of Jekyll's period, is still apparent, sited close to the house.

The position of Jekyll's rose garden which I have illustrated is open to question. At present there is a small rose garden set into the terrace behind the house and facing the main gardens. But, although the shapes of the rose beds appear to be the same as those on Jekyll's plan, the scale of the garden is too diminutive for the generous display of roses proposed by Jekyll. A more likely site is where a large and now unused swimming pool was built by previous owners of Henley Park. The area is large enough to accommodate the complex pattern of beds shown on Jekyll's plan and the setting between sloping banks, enclosed by trees and shrubs, accords exactly with the one drawn out by Jekyll. Even the series of steps leading down or up to the garden are in the same position that they have on the plans.

This would also have been a perfect site for a rose garden. It would have been protected by its cordon of shrubs and trees from the wind which would otherwise affect a garden set in such a high, exposed position. I believe that Jekyll would have chosen this setting for roses. She campaigned in her writing for a more imaginative approach to siting rose gardens and she particularly favoured a background of trees to bring out the colour of the blooms: 'If a Rose garden is to be made on a level space where any artificial alteration of the ground is inexpedient, it will be found a great enhancement to the beauty of the Roses and to the whole effect of the garden if it is so planned that dark shrubs and trees bound it on all sides' (*Roses for English Gardens*). The enclosure of the site would also have ensured that the scents of the roses, brought out by the warmth of a fine summer day, remained in the garden to be enjoyed along with the beauty of the rose blooms.

The formal rose-bed layout is one which Jekyll often adopted with L-shaped beds forming the four corners around a central square bed. The corner beds are planted with hybrid tea or hybrid perpetual roses and the central squares are planted with China roses. Jekyll does not specify which China rose she wished to be planted in this position or whether there should be a mixture of varieties. I have chosen the 'Parson's Pink China' now named 'Old Blush', which was one of the earliest China roses and one familiar to Jekyll. These square beds are edged with stachys and at all four corners there are clumps of acanthus. Curiously there is no indication on Jekyll's plan of a repeat of this edging defining the other formal rose beds.

The formal rose-bed colour scheme was, typically, carefully considered: Jekyll chose a central heart of rich red roses with a softer surround of pinks and whites blushed with pink or tinted with a creamy yellow. The centrally placed roses are sited in four beds – two beds of 'Gruss an Teplitz', which is still available from rose growers, and the

XXXI. Henley Park Sunken Rose Garden

The formal layout of roses planned for this Oxfordshire garden consisted of L-shaped beds forming four corners around two square beds. The colour scheme was carefully conceived to create a central heart of red roses surrounded by pink and blush whites. Roses also feature

among a variety of shrubs and perennial plants on the banks surrounding the formal garden. Jekyll's favourite Scotch briars, *Rosa virginiana*, 'Blush Damask' and 'Jersey Beauty' are planted among broom, weigela, *Cassinia fulvida* and *Hebe brachysiphon*. Pinks, lavenders, dwarf phlox, valerians and cerastium spill over the stone edging containing the bank borders. A sheltered seat is at the far end of the garden.

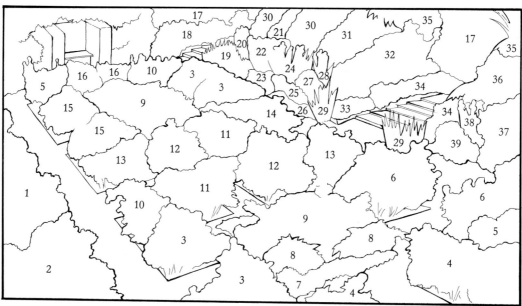

Henley Park Rose Garden (pages 118–19)

1. *Rosa lucida (Rosa virginiana.* I have shown the double form 'Rose d'Amour').
2. Berberis = could be *Berberis aquifolium (Mahonia aquifolium).*
3. Rose 'Frau Karl Druschki' (HT).
4. Rose 'Captain Christy' (HT), deep pink [* 'Mrs. John Laing'].
5. Rose 'Zéphirine Drouhin' (HT).
6. Rose 'Augustine Guinoisseau' (HT).
7. Stachys = *Stachys olympica* (syn. *S. byzantina*).
8. Acanthus = *Acanthus spinosus.*
9. China roses = 'Old Blush'.
10. Rose 'Mme Abel Chatenay' (HT).
11. Rose 'Marquis of Salisbury' (HT), crimson [* 'Marchioness of Salisbury': ◊ 'Crimson Glory'].
12. Rose 'Gruss an Teplitz' (HT).
13. Rose 'Mrs. W. J. Grant' (HT), light pink [* 'Lady Mary Fitzwilliam': ◊ 'Royal Highness'].
14. Rose 'Mme Caroline Testout' (HT), pink [* 'Home Sweet Home'].
15. Rose 'Mme Laurette Messimy' (China).
16. Rose 'Viscountess Folkestone' (HT), cream-white/blush [* 'Ophelia', 'Margaret Merrill'].
17. Rose 'Blush Gallica' ('Blush Damask').
18. Santolina = *Santolina chamaecyparissus.*
19. Dwarf lavender = *Lavandula angustifolia* 'Hidcote' (syn. *L. nana atropurpurea*).
20. Iris = tall bearded iris – 'Vainquer', purple bicolour [* 'Joanna', 'Wabash', 'Maisie Lowe', 'Mrs. J. E. Gibson': ◊ 'Persian Gown'].
21. Pink ulex. [It is unclear what Jekyll had in mind since ulex – gorse – is yellow.]

22. Centranthus = *Centranthus ruber.*
23. *Phlox stellaria* [* Phlox 'G. F. Wilson'].
24. Iris = tall beared iris – 'Vincent', blue bicolour blend [* 'Amigo', 'Braithwaite' and same hybrids as 'Vainquer': ◊ 'Proud Tradition', 'Best Bet', 'Glistening Icicle', 'Nordic Seas', 'River Hawk'; or 'Persian Gown', purple bicolour].
25. Cerastium.
26. *Plumbago larpentae* [*Ceratostigma plumbaginoides*].
27. Veratrum = *Veratrum nigrum.*
28. Iris = tall beared iris – 'Sans Souci', red bicolour [* 'Grace Sturtevant', 'Queechee', 'Solid Mahogany': ◊ 'Chocolate Shake', 'Cayenne Pepper', 'Hell's Fire', 'Play with Fire'].
29. Iris [unspecified. Could be *Iris unguicularis*].
30. *Veronica traversii* (Hebe brachysiphon).
31. *Cassinia fulvida.*
32. Rose 'Jersey Beauty'.
33. Megasea (Bergenia = *B. cordifolia*).
34. White pinks.
35. Yellow broom = *Cytisus scoparius.*
36. Weigela = *Weigela florida.*
37. Scotch briars (*Rosa pimpinellifolia*).
38. Iris = tall bearded iris – 'Bridesmaid', white self [* 'Cliffs of Dover', 'White City', 'New Snow', 'Snowy Owl', 'Winter Olympics': ◊ 'Lacy Snowflake', 'Laced Cotton', 'Pontiff', 'Leda's Lover', 'Skier's Delight'].
39. Pink pinks.

Note: I have suggested alternatives for 'Mme Caroline Testout' and 'Captain Christy' because today these roses are only available as climbers and not as bush roses.

other two of a crimson hybrid tea named 'Marquis of Salisbury' which is no longer grown. The pink roses include the familiar 'Zéphirine Drouhin' and 'Mme. Caroline Testout', together with 'Mme. Abel Chatenay', the delicately pretty China rose, 'Mme. Laurette Messimy' and the rosy-white 'Augustine Guinoisseau', described as a white version of the famous old rose 'La France'. These roses can all still be obtained from specialist rose growers. 'Mrs. W. J. Grant' is not represented on current rose lists and 'Captain Christy' is now only grown as a climber. 'Frau Karl Druschki' is still available but the other white rose marked on the plan, the cream-tinted 'Viscountess Folkestone', is another casualty of time.

Jekyll's sensitivity to colour and its effect on the eye must have inspired the design of the formal bedding area with its core of rich rosy red roses. The pinks and tinted whites in the other beds give a softened outline to the design and successfully blend the formal area into the informal planting of the sloping banks and shrubbery. Here Jekyll has also included roses among the other plants and this creates visual continuity with the formal part of the garden. On one side of the garden there is a liberal planting of *Rosa virginiana* and I have chose to illustrate the double form which Jekyll recommends in *A Gardener's Testament*: 'There is a delightful double form with the old name Rose d'Amour, very beautiful in bud, and more disposed to grow into shapely bushes than the more robust single form'. In this sheltered position I am sure she would have chosen this little rose. The opposite bank is planted with her favourite Scotch briars (*Rosa pimpinellifolia*) and two plantings of 'Blush Damask'. She also suggested 'Jersey Beauty' to tumble down the bank into a waterfall of single yellow blooms. This wichuraiana hybrid was a favourite and Jekyll often used it for this purpose.

The shrubs planted on the banks include weigela, broom, *Cassinia fulvida* and *Hebe brachysiphon*. Berberis is also marked on the plan but I believe this to be *Mahonia aquifolium* which Jekyll referred to as *Berberis aquifolium*. The slightly raised stone edges containing these bank borders are edged with lavender, pinks, dwarf phlox, valerian and cerastium – all chalk-loving plants which would thrive in the soil conditions predominant on this part of the Chiltern ridge. One shallow flight of steps leading down into the rose garden was edged with a mass of santolina while the other was planted on either side with white pinks.

The predominantly pink and grey colour scheme of these borders complements the soft pinks and tinted whites of the roses on the outside borders of the formal design. Jekyll also introduced foliage interest among the perennial plants with the sword-like spikes of iris and bold ridged leaves of veratrum. The whole effect of the planting could be enjoyed from a seat at one end of the garden which was sheltered by a surround of hedging.

Jekyll does not indicate whether she expected the sunken section of the rose garden to be grassed or paved. The present surround to the swimming pool which now occupies the site is partly paved and also partly grassed. I have chosen to show the area paved in common with many other Jekyll rose gardens.

Chapter Eleven

Climbers in the Garden

ONE OF THE MOST DELIGHTFUL PHOTOGRAPHS I have seen of *Clematis montana* was taken by Jekyll: it shows this plant trained in looped garlands on the wall of her house. Her ingenious use of climbing plants is yet another example of the way in which she combined her talents as a gardener and as an artist. Her keen eye observed the many beautiful effects that were often created, as if by chance, in some modest cottage garden where a vine was allowed to embower the whole building and an old quince was left to flourish and produce its fruit under the cottage parlour window.

She tried to inspire her readers to use climbers in a more imaginative way for 'when one sees climbing plants or any of the shrubs that are so often used as climbers, planted in the usual way, about four feet apart and with no attempt at arrangement, it gives one that feeling of regret for opportunities lost or misused' (*Colour in the Flower Garden*). She regretted that her own garden lacked 'a bit of rocky hill-side' for 'there would be the place for the yellow winter Jasmine, for the Honeysuckles both bushy and rambling, for the trailing Clematises... and for the native *C. vitalba*, beautiful both in flower and fruit; for shrubs like *Forsythia suspensa* and *Desmodium penduliflorum*, that like to root high and then throw down cascades of bloom, and for wichuraiana Roses, also for Gourds and wild Vines'.

Jekyll's description of this Surrey hanging garden exemplifies how in her mind's eye she could conjure up an exciting picture made up of plants. Her use of climbers could be daring, involving a complex scheme of planting for a pergola; but it could also rely on a simple but clever association of foliage or a mixture of berries and flowers. It might only take a few plants to create the picture. Her ideas for the use of climbers came from her acute observation of these plants in the wild. The woods and hedges were her inspiration, where honeysuckles could be seen climbing high into the trees, wild clematis wreathing an entire hedge in its delicate flowers and the native hop producing its annual rampant growth.

It was her desire to recreate the natural habit of wild plants which led her to suggest such a variety of ways for using climbers in gardens. She suggested planting clematis at the foot of a tree so that it could twine upwards and flower among the branches just as it did in the wild. The lack of regimentation in nature, where plants never grow up at equal distances from each other and where a gentle form of anarchy prevails, provided Jekyll with endless opportunities of storing new plant pictures in her mind for use in the gardens which she designed.

The interplay of colours between groups of climbing plants in the garden constantly delighted her. In her own garden she admired the picture created by *Clematis flammula*, one of her favourite clematis, intertwined with *Sorbaria lindleyana* (syn. *Sorbaria*

XXXII. Rignall Wood Pergola and Garden House

Rignall Wood Pergola and Garden House (page 123)

1. Plumbago = *Plumbago larpentae* [*Ceratostigma plumbaginoides*].
2. *Alchemilla alpina.*
3. *Silene alpestris.*
4. Welsh poppy = *Meconopsis cambrica.*
5. *Sedum ewersii.*
6. Hart's tongue fern = *Phyllitis scolopendrium* (syn. *Asplenium scolopendrium*).
7. *Campanula carpatica*, white and blue.
8. *Iris stylosa (Iris unguicularis).*
9. Vine = *Vitis vinifera.*
10. Rose 'Blush Rambler'.
11. Rose 'Euphrosyne', pink multiflora [* 'Evangeline'].
12. Vine chasselas = *Vitis chasselas.*
13. *Clematis flammula.*
14. Rose 'Aimée Vibert'.
15. Virginia creeper = *Parthenocissus quinquefolia.*
16. Fig.
17. Aristolochia = *Aristolochia durior.*
18. *Vitis coignetiae.*
19. *Clematis montana.*
20. China rose.

tomentosa), where the bloom of the clematis which had 'the warm white of foam' complemented the light green fern-like leaves of the sorbaria. This same clematis provided her with yet another inspiring combination of colours when she observed 'the foam-like masses of the Clematis resting on the dusky richness of the yew'. Combinations of colour and texture were another source of delight; the 'tender lavender colour' of *Abutilon vitifolium* which harmonized perfectly with its soft downy foliage; the Morning Glory 'Heavenly Blue' winding through a vine providing a vivid contrast between the clear blue of the flowers and the light yellow green of the leaves: 'To my eye it is the most enjoyable colour-feast of the year' (*Colour in the Flower Garden*).

In many of the plans which I have studied, Jekyll even used climbers to great effect in her herbaceous borders, where *Clematis flammula* and *Clematis* 'Jackmanii' were planted behind early flowering perennials such as delphiniums, so that the clematis could colonise these plants when they had finished flowering, covering them in clematis blooms during late summer. In this way the flowering season of the borders was extended. Just as climbing roses could be used to cover an ugly garden building, so Jekyll suggested climbers for the same purpose. She also recommended them to soften the hard angles of a wall, to fall over a bank or terrace wall, or to cover a screen or pergola in curtains of foliage and a mass of blooms.

The architectural Italian pergola was a late introduction to England but, once adopted, it became an important and substantial feature of many Edwardian gardens. Jekyll included it in many of her schemes. The readers of her articles were given useful advice and instructions on how to construct and build a pergola with solid brick or stone piers and cross beams of timber over which a variety of plants could climb, eventually creating a roof of foliage mixed with seasonal flowers.

The pergola at Rignall Wood (see Chapter Three), with its delightful garden house at one end, is one of the finest examples that I have seen in a Jekyll garden and, although it may not be planted out with the original climbers, it has still been maintained and planted so that its period character has been preserved. Both the pergola and garden house are original, with the possible exception of the timber cross-beams which have probably been replaced. The timber pillars on either side of the garden house door are almost certainly ship's timber. The owner of Rignall Wood, Sir Felix Semon, was a friend of the Stewart-Libertys, who owned the famous London shop. Ship's timber had been used for their store in Regent Street, London, and it is believed that there was some left over to provide Felix Semon with these pillars for his garden house.

The painting shows a long perspective view of the pergola as it appears from the flight of steps leading down to the lawn level of the garden. The effect is of a tunnel created by brick piers on one side and a supporting wall on the other, with a luxuriant mass of foliage clinging to timber beams overhead and falling like curtains on either side. The wall slopes back to take the strain of the weight of soil from the upper terrace level. At the far end, one can just see the garden house with its ship's timber pillars flanking the white-painted door, and the red-tiled roof appears between the timber beams of the pergola. A narrow raised border runs along the foot of the wall. Unfortunately there is no planting plan for this border.

I have shown the first flight of steps leading down to the lower level and the planting which Jekyll intended to soften the edges of these steps. The shaded side was planted with hart's tongue fern (*Phyllitis scolopendrium* [syn. *Asplenium scolopendrium*]), Welsh poppy (*Meconopsis cambrica*) and the subtle little *Alchemilla alpina*. The sunny side of the steps provides colour with *Campanula carpatica*, both blue and white, lilac-pink *Sedum ewersii* and white *Silene alpestris*. *Ceratostigma plumbaginoides* with its bright blue flowers clambers down the remaining steps on the sunny side.

The pergola consists of fourteen brick piers with wide spaces in between so that the planting of the lower bank dropping down from the pergola can be seen through generous gaps. This also stops the pergola becoming gloomy or claustrophobic as plenty of light comes in from this side. The planting of this bank was designed by Jekyll to include roses: her favourite 'Mme. Plantier' and China roses. These do not feature in the painting as I have taken a straight view looking down the pergola. The climbers which Jekyll chose were all ones which she recommended for this purpose in her articles and books, and they were designed to give interest throughout the seasons either through their foliage or blooms. Each month would have had its display with the variety of leaf shape and colour providing its own beauty. I have shown the pergola in late summer when the creamy blooms of *Clematis flammula* were the dominant interest. Jekyll often photographed this favourite clematis: 'It takes the form of flowery clouds... this clematis has many other uses, for bowers, arches and pergolas' (*Colour in the Flower Garden*). The year would have started with the white or pink flowers of *Clematis montana* and, later, there would have been roses: the early flowering multiflora, 'Euphrosyne' with its massed blooms of bright pink, then 'Blush Rambler' with its tiny shell pink blooms, 'Blush Damask' which produced fuller pink blooms, red 'Reine Olga' and the charming but vigorous noisette, 'Aimée Vibert'. The pipe-shaped blooms of the large-leafed twining aristolochia added their outlandish appeal among the roses. The climbers were planted in such a way that flowering plants punctuated the pergola at carefully planned intervals so that there was interest throughout its length and flowers over a long season in spring and summer. Later in the year russet tints, the reds and golds of vines and Virginia creepers, would give the pergola autumn beauty. Figs with their sculptured leaves provided strong foliage interest for most of the year.

The fig was one of Jekyll's favourite choices for London gardens where it appeared to survive in the polluted and sooty atmosphere of the day. She also suggested Virginia creeper to provide 'ample wall covering' for a city garden. These two plants were used as a background to a small border of plants in an architectural Chelsea garden. I have chosen this example as it shows that Jekyll could plan both for the kind of grand effect created by a long pergola of climbing plants and for a modest but attractive planting scheme using just two effective climbers.

In the Chelsea garden both of these climbers have positive features to recommend them; the fig has its bold leaves and the Virginia creeper its rich autumn colouring. They were part of a planting designed for Wilbraham House, an imposing but rather austere building designed by the architect, Oliver Hill, in 1923 for his client, Ludley Scott M.D.

The four drawings, which are all that remain of Jekyll's original scheme, show that

XXXIII. Climbers in a corner of the garden at Wilbraham House

Virginia creeper and a fig provide cover for the wall of this London garden and create a background of foliage for a mixture of evergreen plants and scarlet dahlias.

this was a particularly awkward site with a long twisting shape extending sideways from the house, avoiding the bulk of Sloane Terrace Mansions and ending up at Sloane Square. The garden is overlooked at the back by a row of small houses and the plans show that screening was once provided by mulberry trees. A further difficulty for Jekyll was created by the architect's limited provision of border space. Most of the beds were sited below the walls and none of them appeared to be wide enough to support a generous display of plants; they would also have suffered from the twin problems of dryness and shade where trees overshadowed the garden.

Photographs taken of the garden in 1926 for a contemporary book on urban gardens show its architectural design. The view taken through the arches of the arcaded loggia displays the strong pattern of shadows cast by the terraces and this serves to emphasize the structured character of the landscaping. Today, the layout appears to have remained unchanged. The garden is still paved and there are circular steps leading down from each of the shallow terraces marking a change of level in the garden.

These contemporary photographs are too indistinct to show whether the garden was planted out as Jekyll intended, and the personality of the architect seems so firmly imprinted on its design that only the most architectural style of planting would have worked satisfactorily. My painting shows a small border in the autumn with the fig and Virginia creeper planted to soften an awkward angle between two walls by disguising it with their foliage. In my painting the fig is shown with its leaves just beginning to turn yellow and the creeper's leaves are reddening into their autumn colour. Jekyll probably anticipated that the creeper would pick up the bright red of her favourite *Dahlia* 'Fire King'. These two plants provide the only colour in the border except for the various greens.

Jekyll had wisely concentrated on evergreens for this little planting scheme. Her choice may have been partly dictated by the cultural limitations of a contemporary London garden, but she had also selected plants with positive shapes and distinctive leaves so that they would enhance the architectural character of the garden. The painting shows the shiny, deeply cut leaves of *Acanthus spinosus*, the rich green foliage of bergenia and the polished cyclamen-like leaves of *Asarum europaeum*. The cooler blue-green spikes of *Iris pallida-dalmatica* still provide foliage interest even though the plant has finished flowering. *Lilium candidum* is also planted in the border and, during its flowering season, the elegant white blooms, so favoured by Jekyll, would have added their sculptured beauty to the border.

Simple elegance was also the effect that Jekyll would have achieved in her planting of the cloister garden at Brambletye in Sussex. Brambletye is an impressive stone building with an imposing tower and a style of architecture which would not look out of place in Scotland. It dates from 1870 and remained in the Nevill family until 1932. Jekyll was commissioned through the architects Forbes & Tait for their client, Mrs. Guy Nevill. This was Jekyll's third garden for these architects.

The architects' scheme for the grounds, of which nineteen plans remain combining both Jekyll's planting designs, produced in 1919, and the architects' drawings, was elaborate and would have involved an immense amount of work and building. Most of this was to be concentrated at the back of the house where a paved walk running along the length of a sunny upper terrace was to be extended along the top of arcaded cloisters. These structures projected out at right angles to the east and west, flanking a generous sized lawn. The northern end of the lawn was to be enclosed by a long curving pergola. The final effect which the architects hoped to create was of a perfect cloister garden surrounded on all sides by elegant buildings. However, to achieve this effect, which also involved a double drop of terrace walling close to the back of the house, it would have been necessary, in my opinion, to excavate the site. There is no evidence that the cloister garden was ever made and the Nevills may have felt that the

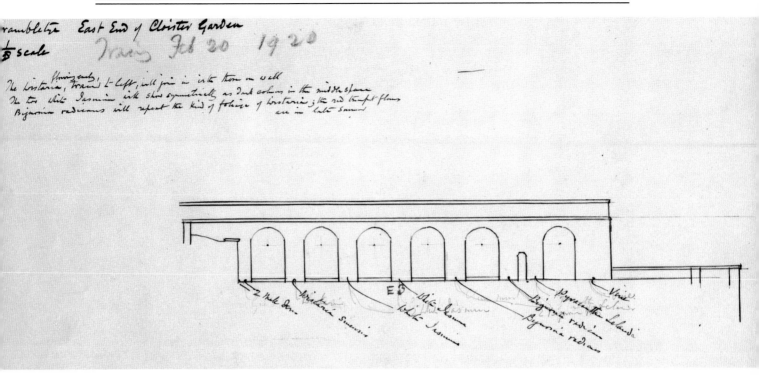

Jekyll's plan for the east end of Brambletye cloister garden

cost and upheaval of creating it was just too much for them to undertake.

Brambletye is now a well-known preparatory school and, although new school buildings obscure much of the original gardens, the house and what remains of the formal gardens still have a superb setting with wonderful views over the surrounding countryside. At the back of the house, where the cloister garden was to be sited, the gardens seem to have remained unaltered and appear much as they did before Forbes & Tait proposed their new design for the grounds. None of the cloister arcades was constructed here and what was intended to be the cloister garden lawn drops down to quite a shallow level which allows for only one depth of terrace wall. It is, however, planted along its length with wisteria, just as it appears on Jekyll's plans.

The view from the lawn must be much as it was before Jekyll produced her new designs for the grounds, for fine old trees stand in exactly the same positions that they occupy on her plans for an extension to the formal gardens. These included planting plans for two magnificent curved herbaceous borders which were intended for the area in front of these trees but which have now been grassed over.

Although it was obviously never built, I have chosen to paint the east end of the cloister garden: here Jekyll's elegant choice of climbers, perfectly complementing the stonework of the arcaded cloister, is a good example of her ability to produce a basically simple arrangement of plants which were ideal for their setting. The Forbes & Tait plans show a stretch of wall with arches which presumably led into the arcade of the cloister. The drawings are not absolutely clear but one may assume that a cloister garden would have had a covered walk.

XXXIV. Brambletye Cloister Garden

The elegant arcade planned in 1919 for the grounds of this Sussex house, now a preparatory school, was probably never built. It was part of an ambitious scheme to construct arcades on two sides of a central lawn. A double drop of terrace wall was planned for the third side and

a long pergola, forming the fourth side, completely enclosed the lawn, thus creating a perfect cloister garden. The painting shows the arcade planned for one side of the garden clothed in climbing plants. In the left foregound is jasmine, followed by *Campsis radicans, Pyrancantha coccinea* 'Lalandei' and finally, to the right of the picture, the vine, *Vitis vinifera* 'Purpurea'.

Jekyll must have given a great deal of practical thought to her choice of climbers for the Brambletye cloister. In *Gardens for Small Country Houses* she warned her readers against the 'injudicious use of climbing plants' by which she meant the indiscriminate planting of vigorous plants like ivy against masonry. She pointed out that, particularly with old crumbling mortar, woody climbers could get a firm purchase between stone or brickwork after which, in a surprisingly short period of time, the hard swelling shoots of ivy could prise stones or bricks apart causing great damage to the structure of the building. However, Jekyll advised her readers that ivy was a beautiful plant if used correctly, for example 'as screening walls of greenery on railings or treillage'. *Ampelopsis veitchii* (*Parthenocissus tricuspidata* 'Veitchii') was another culprit responsible for doing serious harm to brickwork: Jekyll particularly mentions its smothering and eroding effect on the old Tudor buildings of Hampton Court.

Jekyll was also concerned with an aesthetic consideration. A single plant allowed to cover a large area could appear dull unless other climbers were combined with it to create an interesting association of foliage. Although a characterless building could be greatly enhanced by a covering of climbers, a fine piece of architecture with distinguished features should have these adequately displayed and not disguised by too thick a blanket of monotonous leafage. The aim was to create an attractive picture, pleasing to the eye and achieving a carefully designed balance between masonry and foliage. Thus Jekyll's selection for the Brambletye cloister excluded over-invasive plants and the arcade was intended to be attractively clothed with an interesting combination of climbers.

I have shown Jekyll's planting scheme in September as her choice of plants suggests that they were planned to give a fine autumn display. The climbers were to be planted in between the arches of the arcade. Jekyll's notes on the plan indicate that she eventually expected all the climbers to combine and join together, leaving only the archways free from foliage. She started at the south end of the cloister with a vine. The variety is unspecified, so I have shown the vine she used so often, *Vitis vinifera* 'Purpurea'. Next to it was planted *Pyracantha coccinea* 'Lalandei', followed by two plantings of *Campsis radicans*, the scarlet flowered trumpet vine. The next two arches were to be planted with 'the common but always delightful white Jasmine'. The last two arches are out of my picture, so I have not been able to show the wisteria that was to be planted there and which was intended to join up with and become part of a fine display of wisteria designed for the whole length of the terrace wall at the back of the house.

The painting shows the arcade as it would have appeared when the planting was mature. The bright berries of the pyracantha, the red trumpets of the campsis and the claret autumn tints of the vine stand out against the grey stone of the arcade which I have matched to the stone of the house. The white jasmine would not have been at its best but, once well established, would still have been in bloom at this time of year.

Chapter Twelve

Woodland Gardens

'THE WOODLAND WALK is not the place for masses of showy flowers, it is rather for solitary sauntering and the leisurely refreshment of a quiet mind' (*Wall, Water and Woodland Gardens*). The natural beauty of woodland with its subtle and unplanned effects had a haunting appeal for Jekyll. She wrote lyrically of wooded pathways and lanes where she observed the changes that each month and season of the year imposed on native trees and plants.

In this peaceful environment, her artist's eye observed the subdued beauty of colour effects created by the relationship between wood and foliage where patterns of light and shade added variety among a limited range of colours. These quiet periods of reflection and observation enabled Jekyll to concentrate her attention on combinations of woodland plants and their colours, thereby enabling her to perceive as an artist what an untrained eye would find hard to see and appreciate:

The untrained eye only sees colour as it is locally. I suppose any one who has never gone through this kind of training could scarcely believe the difference it makes in the degree of enjoyment of all that is most worthy of admiration in our beautiful world. But it enables one, even in a greater degree than the other perceptions of form and proportion that the artist must acquire or cultivate, to see pictures for oneself, not merely to see objects. (*Home and Garden*)

In *Wood and Garden*, she records her observations of woodland throughout the seasons. Even during the bleak winter months, she found colour effects which entranced her and unexpected richness of tones, patterns and shapes which would provide her with inspiration and heightened sensitivity when she planned her colour schemes of cultivated plants:

The ground has a warm carpet of pale rusty fern; tree-stem and branch and twig show tender colour-harmonies of grey bark and silver-grey lichen, only varied by the warm feathery masses of birch spray. Now the splendid richness of the common holly is more than ever impressive, with its solid masses of full, deep colour... The picture is made complete by the slender shafts of the silver-barked birches... The tints of the stem give a precious lesson in colour. The white of the bark is here silvery-white and there milk-white, and sometimes shows the faintest tinge of rosy flush. Where the bark has not yet peeled, the stem is clouded and banded with delicate grey, and with the silver-grey of lichen.

Jekyll's ability to memorize delicate colour effects and intricate arrangements of woodland plants made it possible for her to reproduce the natural landscaping and planting of woodland in the semi-cultivated woodland gardens which she designed for her clients. Her own piece of woodland at Munstead Wood was also an invaluable trial ground where she could experiment and gain experience before planning other wild gardens, most of which she would never have the advantage of visiting.

To unite a formal garden to woodland, so that there would not be a 'sudden jolt' to the eye where trees and garden met too abruptly, presented a design problem which Jekyll had found unresolved in many contemporary gardens. Her own suggestion was to leave a generous space between wood and garden: this was to be landscaped and laid out with appropriate shrubs and plants so that the margins between cultivated garden and woodland were bridged harmoniously. Instead of planting in geometric borders, Jekyll tried to imitate the grouping of native plants which she had observed growing in the wild. She designed layouts where formal borders were replaced by islands and drifts of shrubs and plants interwoven with paths which looped their way round the planting and eventually led into the woodland beyond.

Viewed from above or seen on her plans, there was a fluid rhythm to the pattern of these paths as they wove among the islands of shrubs. This type of layout was repeatedly used by Jekyll for her wild gardens. Where access to the woodland area was reached through formal gardens, Jekyll stressed that the character of the paths should change by degrees as they led further into woodland. Paths winding in between groups of rhododendrons at the margin between lawn and trees should be made of turf to blend with the grass of the lawn, but once into woodland, the paths should remain unmade and natural with only the most invasive brambles or treacherous roots removed to ensure a clear passage.

Rhododendrons were frequently used by Jekyll to bridge the gap between formal gardens and woodland:

Among the various ways of passing from garden to woodland one of the best is by planting Rhododendron . . . For the best effect it will be well that the Rhododendrons shall begin with some of tender colouring, pale and rich pink, following on to good reds. For this they could begin with such as Pink Pearl and Alice, passing on to rosy reds such as Lady Eleanor Cathcart and Mrs. R.S. Holford. (*Wall, Water and Woodland Gardens*)

My painting shows a good example of Jekyll planting under a canopy of light woodland at Walsham House (see Chapter Eight) with grass paths weaving in between clumps of rhododendrons. The woodland extends from a grassed area planted out with groups of shrubs, where there is still evidence of a Jekyll rock garden with an attractive watercourse that drops down through different levels.

Three of the rhododendrons which Jekyll particularly recommends are included in my painting. 'Pink Pearl' is in the left foreground as one looks at the picture. Beyond is the lilac-flowered and fragrantly scented azaleodendron 'Odoratum' and also the rosy-bloomed 'Mrs. R. S. Holford'. On the right, in the background, the white flushed-pink flowers of 'Baroness Henry Schroder' and the deep pink blooms of 'Lady Longman' can be glimpsed between the trees. The paths seen in my picture are edged with *Leucothoë axillaris*, whereas elsewhere in the woodland the leucothoë gives way to generous plantings of lady fern. The painting shows the woodland in May.

Azaleas and in particular the Ghent hybrids were also suggested by Jekyll for planting under trees or on the margins of woodland, but she felt that they should be kept

XXXV. Rhododendrons in Woodland, Walsham House

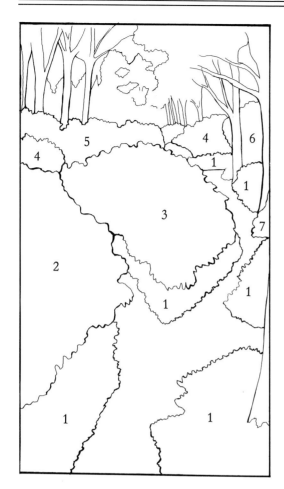

Rhododendrons in Woodland,
Walsham House (page 135)

1. *Andromeda axillaris* [*Leucothoë axillaris*].
2. *Rhododendron* 'Pink Pearl'.
3. *Rhododendron* 'Alice'.
4. *Azaleodendron odoratum*, lilac [Grown from seed of *Azalea viscosum* planted close to *Rhododendron ponticum*: ◊ *Rh.* 'Azaleoides', grown from seed from *Azalea periclymenoides*].
5. *Rhododendron* 'Mrs. R. S. Holford'.
6. *Rhododendron* 'Baroness Henry Schroder', white flushed magenta-pink [* Mrs. Furnival'].
7. *Rhododendron* 'Lady Longman'.

separate from the shrubberies of rhododendron. She maintained that although there was a close family relationship between these shrubs, their habit and, perhaps more significantly, their colours were not compatible. Jekyll also warned against planting azaleas in groups of different varieties without consideration for their individual habits and colours. She describes in *Wood and Garden* the carefully planned sequence of colours she followed when planting azaleas at Munstead Wood:

The whites are planted at the lower and more shady end of the group; next come the pale yellows and pale pinks, and these are followed at a little distance by kinds whose flowers are of orange, copper, flame, and scarlet-crimson colourings; this strong coloured group again softening off at the upper end by strong yellows, and dying away into the woodland by bushes of the common yellow *Azalea pontica*, and its variety with flowers of larger size and deeper colour.

At Stilemans (see Chapter Eight), where a woodland garden was one of the features which Jekyll designed for the grounds, the shrubberies of azaleas when in full bloom were described to me enthusiastically by the head gardener as 'just like flames under the trees'. Although these azaleas may not be the original plants, their blend of colours, which harmonize to produce such an effective display, appears to have been maintained to emulate Jekyll's original scheme.

Vacciniums, kalmias, cistus and *Gaultheria shallon*, the suckering little shrub which can still be found growing in some Jekyll woodland gardens, were also used by Jekyll. Apart from shrubs, she recommended a variety of plants which would blend sympathetically into the environment of a wood or wild garden.

Ferns were among Jekyll's choice of plants for wild gardening and she drew on experience of her own fern garden at Munstead Wood. The lady fern, *Athyrium filix-femina*, which Jekyll regarded as one of the most graceful of native ferns, was suggested for damp ground; the hart's tongue fern, *Phyllitis scolopendrium* (syn. *Asplenium scolopendrium*), for cool shade where it would benefit from soil enriched with leaf-mould. She also recommended the northern hard fern, *Blechnum spicant*, and the grand royal fern, *Osmunda regalis*, which was to be planted individually rather than in groups so that each fern could be appreciated as a single specimen. Trillium, Solomon's Seal and wild subjects like cardamine, uvularia, woodruff and white foxgloves formed compatible partnerships with ferns which were to be planted in 'handsome masses' among the other plants.

One of Jekyll's favourite plants for planting in wild or woodland gardens were primroses. She had, over the years, developed her own strain of polyanthus, which she referred to as the Munstead Bunch Primroses, and the photographs which she took of them in her own garden show how she arranged these plants in great sweeping drifts with narrow pathways in between, which led through the plants and into woodland.

Clearings between the trees where there was only light shade provided Jekyll with a 'precious opportunity' for planting daffodils, either in drifts of one variety or, where space was generous, in a sequence of drifts beginning with the common narcissi and continuing with a range of its various hybrids. Of the smaller bulbs, Jekyll recommended planting scillas, rather than the more invasive native bluebell, in semi-cultivated woodland.

Varieties of lilies were recommended for the margins of woodland: *Lilium auratum*, *Lilium croceum* and the tiger lily, *Lilium tigrinum*. But Jekyll derived the greatest pride from her successful cultivation of a plant which she refers to as *Lilium giganteum* or the giant lily. Jekyll's photograph of this impressive plant in *Wood and Garden* shows it being closely scrutinized by a mysterious figure wearing a monk's habit. These robes, borrowed from a Sussex monastery, hid the identity of Jekyll's gardener who, presumably, had agreed to pose in this disguise specially for the photograph. The giant lily has today been re-classified as *Cardiocrinum giganteum* and I have made it the subject of my small painting showing it planted among a drift of lady fern in woodland, one of the features which Jekyll included in her scheme of wild planting for Walsham House.

Although some of the rhododendrons at Walsham House may date back to Jekyll's planting scheme, little else appears to remain of her planting for this piece of Surrey woodland. It is in the character of wild gardens to revert back to nature, quickly reclaimed by invasive native plants, because they are not cultivated like formal gardens. But they too need constant care and attention if they are to remain 'a pleasure to the eye'.

XXXVI. *Cardiocrinum giganteum* in woodland, Walsham House

Jekyll was proud of her success in cultivating the 'giant lily', shown here planted among lady fern beside a curving path through woodland in Surrey.

The circumstances of her life had required that Jekyll should imagine and create pictures, not with canvas and paints, but with gardens and plants – a medium which was fragile, transient and difficult to control. She had to visualise her garden pictures three-dimensionally, a more exacting process than painting them on flat canvas; and she had to imagine a fresh palette of plants for every season of the year, for her pictures had to be designed to change and evolve with the passage of time. Whereas an artist can reasonably suppose that a painting, with some care, will last several generations, a garden requires constant attention and maintenance; the neglect of even a few weeks quickly shows. It is therefore not surprising that so much of Jekyll's work has been lost and can now only be appreciated in a few gardens or by studying her plans. If this book has brought some gardens back to life in my paintings and revived interest in the fate of Jekyll's other lost gardens, it will have fulfilled its purpose.

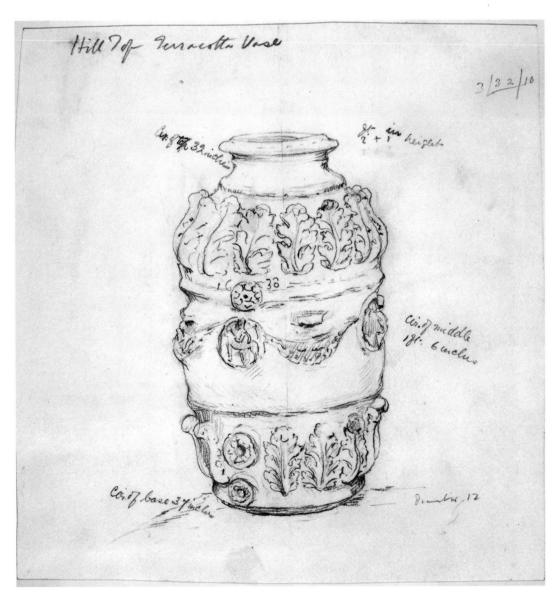

Jekyll's design for a terracotta vase

Bibliography

Birren, Faber, *The Principles of Harmony and Contrast of Colours and their Application to the Arts by M. E. Chevreul* (New York, Reinhold, 1967).

Brown, Jane, *Gardens of a Golden Afternoon* (Penguin Books, 1985).

Henslow, T. Geoffrey W., *The Rose Encyclopaedia* (C. Arthur Pearson Ltd., 1922).

Jekyll, Francis, *Gertrude Jekyll, A Memoir* (Jonathan Cape, 1934).

Jekyll, Gertrude, *Wood and Garden* (Longmans Green, 1899).

    Home and Garden (Longmans Green, 1900).

    Wall and Water Gardens (Newnes/Country Life, 1901).

    Roses for English Gardens with Edward Mawley (Newnes/Country Life, 1902).

    Some English Gardens with paintings by George S. Elgood (Longmans Green, 1904).

    Colour in the Flower Garden (Newnes/Country Life, 1908).

    Children and Gardens (Newnes/Country Life, 1908).

    Gardens for Small Country Houses, with Lawrence Weaver (Newnes/Country Life, 1912).

    Wall, Water and Woodland Gardens (Country Life, 1933).

    A Gardener's Testament (Country Life, 1937).

Massingham, Betty, *Portrait of a Great Gardener* (David & Charles, 1973).

McFarland, J. Horace, *Roses of the World in Color* (Cassell & Co. Ltd. 1937).

Sanders, T. W., *Rock Gardens and Alpine Plants* (W. H. & L. Collingridge).

Schnare, Susan and Rudy J. Favretti, *Gertrude Jekyll's American Gardens* (The Journal of The Garden History Society, 1982).

Tankard, Judith and Michael R. Van Valkenburgh, *A Vision of Garden and Wood* (John Murray, 1989).

Thomas, H. H. *The Complete Gardener* (Cassell and Co. Ltd., 1918).

Tooley, Michael J., *Gertrude Jekyll, a Collection of Essays* (Michaelmas Books, 1984).

Catalogues: Turner 1925, Veitch & Sons 1891 – 1895, Ware 1913.

Acknowledgements

I owe my warmest thanks to many people: without their help this book could not have been produced.

I am indebted to the owners and occupiers of the Jekyll gardens. Their enthusiastic cooperation and, in many cases, kind hospitality have left me with many pleasant memories or my visits to their gardens. My thanks are due to Mark Bales, Mr. and Mrs. William Bainbridge, Colonel and Mrs. Robin Bell, The Hon. and Mrs. Christopher Brett, A. Chappel, Mr. and Mrs. David Clive, Mrs. Margareta Cohen, Mr. and Mrs. Peter Collacott, IBM Hursley – Ian Stockdale, Peter Kaye, Baron and Baroness Von Kleinschmidt, Mr. and Mrs. Geoffrey Lawson, Mr. and Mrs. David Mills, Mr. and Mrs. Francis Robinson, Mr. and Mrs. Anthony Rosen, Mr. and Mrs. Donald Fowler-Watt, and the owner of Walsham House.

I have been fortunate in receiving advice from horticultural experts, many of whom are custodians of our National Plant Collections. They have helped me by suggesting alternatives to plants which Gertrude Jekyll featured in her plans but which are no longer available from growers. If I have misinterpreted the advice I have been given, any horticultural errors in this book are my own. I would like to offer my thanks to Jacques Amand (gladioli), Peter Beales (roses – all the alternative roses in this book are available from his nursey: Peter Beales Roses, London Road, Attleborough, Norfolk NR17 1AY), A. R. Busby (heleniums), The Earl of Carnarvon and Douglas Harris (rhododendrons and azaleodendrons), T. E. Exley (phlox), Mark Flanagan (skimmias), P. Hammond (alpines, Cambridge Botanic Gardens), Dr. Kinsman (aconitum), R. H. Jeffs and Peter Maynard (British Iris Society), Graham Pattison (NCCPG, Wisley), Archie Skinner (Ghent azaleas), Audrey Widdison (helianthus). My thanks go to John Elsley of Park Seed/Wayside Gardens for suggesting alternative plants for America: and also to Diana Saville for allowing me to draw freely on her horticultural expertise.

I should also like to thank Derek Baker, Dalton W. Battin, J.R.D. Campbell, Susan R. Chandler (Connecticut Historical Commission), R. Jayne Craven (Public Library of Cincinnati & Hamilton County), Lynda Davies, Nelly Doolan (Jekyll at the Glebe House Committee), Anne Johns (Guildford Library Local Studies Department), Brian MacFarland (Director, The Glebe House), Heather MacKinlay, Clive Warren, May P. Wooding (Wallingford Historical Society, Connecticut), Staff at the Lindley Library, Staff of the Botanical Department, Royal Horticultural Society Gardens, Wisley, Staff at the Royal Commission for Historical Monuments, Staff at Godalming Museum, Staff at Chelsea Library, Staff at Stourbridge Town Hall and Library. Extracts from Miss Jekyll's correspondence and her drawings are reproduced by kind permission of the College of Environmental Design Documents Collection, University of California, Berkeley.

I would also like to thank Anna Kythreotis for taking my photograph for the jacket.

Throughout the time I have worked on this book, my greatest support has come from my husband, Anthony.

Plant index